# EXPLORER'S BIBLE STUDY

# Prophets of Israel

## By Marni Shideler McKenzie

Book 2 - Lessons 11-20

*Ezekiel*
*Daniel*

Explorer's Bible Study
2652 Hwy. 46 South
P.O. Box 425
Dickson, TN 37056-0425
1-615-446-7316
www.explorerbiblestudy.org

## *About the Author*

**Marni Shideler McKenzie** attended the University of Mississippi as a Carrier Scholar and received B.A. and M.A. degrees in English. While in college, Marni became serious in her efforts to nurture her relationship with Jesus Christ and began to study the Bible carefully. In 1974, Marni married William H. Mckenzie III. She "retired" from a brief high school teaching career when their first child was born and has used her spare time ever since for organizing or teaching Bible study classes to adults and children. Marni has written several **Quest** courses for Jr. and Sr. High including **Early History of Israel, Words of Wisdom, Promises Fulfilled, Faith At Work,** and **God's Perfect Plan**. Marni is also the author of five adult curriculum courses: **Judges and Kings of Israel; Prophets of Israel; Romans, Galatians, and James; Hebrews and First Peter;** and **God's Perfect Plan** and co-authored **The Gospel of John**. Marni and Bill make their home in Batesville, Mississippi, where Bill is an attorney in private practice. They have three children, and two of whom are married, and three grandchildren. Marni has been a teaching leader for Explorer's Bible Study since 1979.

© Copyright 2004 by Explorer's Bible Study
All Rights Reserved

2007 Edition; Printed 2015

ISBN 978-1889015-23-1

Cover Design and Original Artwork by Troy D. Russell

All scripture quotations, unless otherwise indicated, are taken from the New King James Version®.
Copyright © 1982 by Thomas Nelson, Inc. Used by permission. All rights reserved.

We believe the Bible is God's Word, a divine revelation, in the original language verbally inspired in its entirety, and that it is the supreme infallible authority in all matters of faith and conduct.
(2 Peter 1:21; 2 Timothy 3:16)

Printed in the United States of America

# PROPHETS OF ISRAEL — LESSON 11

## Daily Bible Study Questions

**Study Procedure:** Read the Scripture references before answering questions. Unless otherwise instructed, use the Bible only in answering questions. Some questions may be more difficult than others but try to answer as many as you can. Pray for God's wisdom and understanding as you study and don't be discouraged if some answers are not obvious at first.

### THIS WEEK'S MEMORY VERSES:

(Ezekiel 16:49,50) *"Look, this was the iniquity of your sister Sodom: She and her daughter had pride, fullness of food, and abundance of idleness; neither did she strengthen the hand of the poor and needy. And they were haughty and committed abomination before Me; therefore I took them away as I saw fit."*

(Ezekiel 18:32) *"For I have no pleasure in the death of one who dies, says the Lord GOD. Therefore turn and live!"*

### FIRST DAY: Review of Ezekiel 7-13; Read Ezekiel 14

1. Why did the glory of the Lord depart from the temple in Jerusalem?

2. How did Ezekiel correct the thinking of those left in Jerusalem about their superiority to their exiled relatives in Babylon?

3. Read Ezekiel 14:1-11. In an earlier vision, Ezekiel had been shown the idolatrous practices of the leaders in Jerusalem.
   (a) What idolatry was revealed here in the leaders with him in exile?

   (b) What was the remedy?

4. Read Ezekiel 14:12-21 and Leviticus 26. How was God going to respond to the *"persistent unfaithfulness"* of Judah?

5. What wrong idea or misconception was God correcting in repeating the thought that if Noah, Daniel, and Job were in the land, they would still only succeed in delivering themselves from judgment and no one else?

# LESSON 11    PROPHETS OF ISRAEL

6. Read Ezekiel 14:22,23. Characterize the remnant who would escape the last judgment on Jerusalem. How would they "comfort" the exiles in Babylon who questioned the righteousness of God's judgment?

**SECOND DAY: Read Ezekiel 15 and 16**

7. Read Ezekiel 15. List several ways in which Jerusalem was like the pruned branches of a vine. (See John 15:5.)

8. Read Ezekiel 16:1-43. This is a shockingly graphic parable about God's assessment of Judah's condition. Matching:
   _____(a) The original inhabitants or "parents" (of Jerusalem) were these.
   _____(b) The cruel conditions surrounding the nation of Israel's birth were these.
   _____(c) The initial act of compassion by God for her was this.
   _____(d) The act of God toward her when she grew up to be of marriageable age was this.
   _____(e) The generosity of God toward His betrothed was shown in His giving her these.
   _____(f) This was the way she misused her gifts, breaking her covenant with her husband.
   _____(g) Though saved from abuse at birth, she coldly did this to her own children.
   _____(h) More depraved than a harlot, she paid these to commit adultery with her.
   _____(i) She was so evil that even these heathen people were ashamed of her lewd behavior.
   _____(j) This punishment would come upon her for her adulteries and idolatries.
   _____(k) Her failure to do this led to the rest of her sins.

   1. embroidered clothing, badger-skin sandals, linens, silks, ornaments, jewelry, and crown
   2. She killed them and offered them by fire to a false god.
   3. Egypt, Assyria, and Chaldea (Babylon)
   4. the Philistines
   5. Amorites and Hittites of Canaan
   6. He gave word that she should live, took her in, washed her, and provided for her care.
   7. She had been abandoned and exposed in her blood, in an open field, right after birth.
   8. She failed to remember God's past mercies towards her.
   9. She would be exposed naked in front of her former lovers and treated as an adulteress: her possessions would be taken and home destroyed by fire; then she would be stoned with stones and cut down with swords.
   10. She used her gifts to make male idol images, her clothes to make tents for harlotry, and her food as offerings to false gods.
   11. He betrothed her to Himself in the covenant of marriage, symbolizing His intention by spreading His garment over her.

# LESSON 11
## PROPHETS OF ISRAEL

9. Read Ezekiel 16:44-59. God said that Jerusalem had become worse than her "sisters" Samaria and Sodom. What had been Sodom's sins? Comment on this in regard to your own nation.

10. Read Ezekiel 16:60-63. Though God's covenant people had betrayed His trust, what did He still promise to provide for them that would leave them speechless?

## THIRD DAY: Read Ezekiel 17

11. God had Ezekiel present a riddle, which was also a parable, to his fellow exiles. Kindly, God also provided the explanation. Read Ezekiel 17:1-21 and answer the following questions. Multiple choice:

    (a) The first great eagle with large wings and various colored feathers was
        1. Jerusalem.  2. Babylon.  3. Egypt.

    (b) The highest branch of the cedar of Lebanon was
        1. Jerusalem.  2. Pharaoh.  3. the king of Judah.

    (c) This is where the great eagle took and planted the highest branch of the cedar.
        1. Babylon  2. Egypt  3. Jerusalem

    (d) The king of Judah's relative who was allowed to take over the throne in Judah acted treacherously in doing this.
        1. sending ambassadors to Egypt when he was supposed to be in covenant with Babylon
        2. killing all his heirs to the throne
        3. stepping down from the throne in protest

    (e) This would be done to that same king of Judah's relative for breaking covenant with Babylon.
        1. He would be imprisoned in Egypt.
        2. He would be taken, tried, and imprisoned in Babylon, with supporters being killed or scattered.
        3. He would be made a slave in Jerusalem.

12. Read 2 Kings 24:12-17 and identify Judah's king (Ezekiel 17:12) and the king's relative (Ezekiel 17:13) depicted in the previous parable.

13. Read Ezekiel 17:22-24. Although Babylon would crush the nation of Judah and seemingly stop the line of David from ruling any more, what did God promise to do in the future to keep the line going? (See Isaiah 4:2 and Zechariah 3:8.)

# LESSON 11
**PROPHETS OF ISRAEL**

## FOURTH DAY: Read Ezekiel 18

14. Read Ezekiel 18:1-2. Explain in your own words what this proverb meant.

15. Although there is certainly some truth in that proverb—see Exodus 20:5—what would happen to your own personal behavior if you believed that the bad things that happened to you were always the result of your parents' bad choices?

16. Read Ezekiel 18:3-18. Summarize the one shared truth of these three illustrations.

17. Read Ezekiel 18:19-31. The people still didn't quite get what God was trying to teach them. What did He want from them individually? Give verses to support your answer.

## FIFTH DAY: Read Ezekiel 19

18. Read Ezekiel 19:1 and the end of verse 14. Consult a dictionary and write out the definition of a lamentation.

19. At the time Ezekiel wrote this lamentation, Judah had not yet fallen to Babylon. This, then, was at least partially prophetic of what was to come. Read Ezekiel 19:2-9 in which Judah was depicted as a lioness bearing cubs. Then read the following passages and describe how Ezekiel's lamentation was actually fulfilled.
    (a) See 2 Kings 23:31-34 for the first cub of verses 2-4.

    (b) See 2 Kings 24:17,18 and 2 Kings 25:1-7 for the other cub of verses 5-9.

20. God used prophecy to warn his people. Read 2 Chronicles 36:11-18. What was the response of the people still in Judah to prophetic warnings such as these from true prophets like Ezekiel?

Page 4

21. Read Ezekiel 19:10-14. Judah was characterized in this section as being God's choice vine. Contrast her beginning with what Ezekiel prophesied to be her future state.
    (a) Beginning

    (b) Future


22. Review this week's Scripture and questions. Write down one or two things that the Holy Spirit has made clear to you. If these require action on your part, what action do you plan to take?

# Ezekiel 14-19

## Hidden Idolatry (Ezekiel 14:1-11)

Previously, through the power of the Holy Spirit, Ezekiel had been shown actual acts of idolatry going on in or near the temple in Jerusalem (Ezekiel 8), but in Ezekiel 14, the Holy Spirit revealed that the elders with him in exile were just as guilty, because they were keeping idols in their hearts. This was a serious matter. Idolatry in the heart was just the seedbed or garden plot from which ungodly actions inevitably would spring forth: *"For as he thinks in his heart, so is he"* (Proverbs 23:7a). That is why God is so concerned with the condition of the human heart, which He can always see perfectly: *"And there is no creature hidden from His sight, but all things are naked and open to the eyes of Him to whom we must give account"* (Hebrews 4:13).

God revealed to Ezekiel the idolatry in the hearts of his listeners not just so he could expose them but also so that he could warn them to repent and turn back to their Lord. The Hebrew word "to repent," which Ezekiel chose to use, was not the more common one which meant only to be sorry for sin. Instead, he used the word that called them to turn around and come back to God by turning away from all their idolatry. Putting God first must be a continual choice, a moment-by-moment decision to be made by all who want His covenant blessings.

What is so serious about idolatry? Idolatry is allowing something or someone other than God to be the motivating force in your life for what you think, what you desire, or what you choose to do. Anything that blocks God's voice from your thinking or keeps God's word from being your authority cannot lead you into any long-term good or provide you any lasting satisfaction or peace anyway. Idolatry ultimately hurts most the one indulging in it.

But how does idolatry get started in our lives? Paul wrote in Romans 1 that it all begins with ingratitude: Ingratitude for the things of God leads to disrespect and disregard for God Himself. The God-void created is quickly filled with idols that only command that we satisfy our personal and selfish needs, making it so easy to serve them. However, unfortunately, as the elders in exile demonstrated, it is possible to maintain an outward reputation for righteousness while secretly serving idols such as popularity, power, or prestige within. Good works and religious activities can be done from wrong motives, but God always sees the difference. If Ezekiel's listeners did not repent but continued, hypocritically, to ask their prophets for fresh news from God while following only their own desires, God would act quickly to punish them. Then, too late, they would know that He is God (Ezekiel 14:8).

## Curses on Covenant-Breakers (Leviticus 26 and Ezekiel 14:12-23)

From the first of the Ten Commandments and throughout the entire Scriptures, God declared His hatred of idolatry. Leviticus 26 began with a listing of blessings on those who stayed away from idolatry, but the chapter ended with a description of the curses that would always fall on those who tried to replace God with idols. The curses were the same ones Ezekiel described: plagues, attacks from enemies, famine, and attacks from wild beasts. God had been warning His people for centuries.

God had Ezekiel point out that the national life of Israel had deteriorated so far at this time, that even if such recognizably righteous men as Noah, Daniel, or Job were present in it, only they would be saved. One of the things God was teaching here was that no one is saved by association with another. A godly mother or father cannot guarantee entrance to heaven for their children. Personal salvation is required. However, righteousness in a minority of people can sometimes cause God to postpone judgment on the larger group for a time. In this situation of Ezekiel's day, however, God was saying that such time was about to run out. Those who had neglected to receive God's offer of covenant redemption would be destroyed, and only the righteous would receive His mercy.

The fact that Daniel was mentioned with Noah and Job trouble some commentators. They doubt that this could be the Daniel of the Bible and try to link the name with some ancient heathen leader described on an archeological carving. However, since Noah and Job were well-known men of the Scriptures noted for their faithfulness to the true God, why should this Daniel not be of the same fame? Daniel was actually a contemporary of Ezekiel's, having been taken to Babylon just a few years ahead of Ezekiel in 605 B.C. during the first exile. Believed to be of royal lineage, he was recognized as a a young man of intelligence, with good potential, and was placed in the palace of Nebuchadnezzar for further training and usefulness to the government. Ezekiel was taken in the second group of exiles to Babylon around 597 B.C. He served his fellow captives outside the palace boundaries. Just as it is common in our day for a person of exceptional talent or accomplishment in one area—perhaps a pro-athlete, a best-selling author, a popular actor, or an anointed preacher—to keep up with others in the same field, it is quite believable that Ezekiel could have kept up with his brother-in-the-faith Daniel who was making news for his righteous activities in the court of Nebuchadnezzar. Daniel certainly deserved to be in the same class as Noah and Job.

## A Worthless Vine (Ezekiel 15)

God offered a visual aid to Ezekiel to help explain what was about to happen to Jerusalem. Using the commonly seen vine as His example, God asked what use a cut branch of it was for any practical purpose. Then He answered His own question. God told Ezekiel that it was good for nothing, not even for making a peg on which to hang things. A severed branch was destined only to be fuel for the fire. So it was to be with those in Jerusalem: Severed from their covenant relationship with God because of their persistent unfaithfulness (Ezekiel 15:8), God was sending them into the fires of judgment. God's assessment of the condition of broken-off branches was echoed much later in Jesus' teaching to His disciples in John 15:5,6:

*"I am the vine, you are the branches. He who abides in Me, and I in him, bears much fruit; for without Me you can do nothing. If anyone does not abide in Me, he is cast out as a branch and is withered; and they gather them and throw them into the fire, and they are burned."*

## R-Rated Rebuke (Ezekiel 16:1-43)

This frank assessment of the wickedness of God's people can make a person blush! While Hosea's writings described Israel as foolishly promiscuous, unaware, and misled, Ezekiel's record revealed a picture of Israel as a woman indulging in perversion, sickeningly ungrateful for the chance at the good life she had been given. In graphic terms, God described her beginning, when she was cast off at birth, bloody and abandoned, to die of exposure. He saw her, pitied her, rescued her, and caused her to live. Not only that, but when she matured, He married her, providing richly for every need and desire. Fine clothes, beautiful jewelry, and abundant food were given to her. She was admired by many, but her own beauty deceived her. Instead of remaining faithful to the husband who had loved her, even when she had been most unlovely, she began to play the whore indiscriminately for anyone who was willing. She even used the gifts given by her lawful husband to promote her sinful ways, forgetting the condition from which she had been rescued.

Not content to stay near home, Israel played the harlot with Egypt, Assyria, and finally Chaldea. Her behavior made even the heathen Philistines blush (Ezekiel 16:27). Worse than a prostitute who might have justified her behavior as necessary to procure money to pay her way in troubled times, Israel did not need the money but paid others to let her be a harlot, being more perverse than the common prostitute.

God had had enough. She had shamed Him for the last time. God would assemble her former lovers to see her nakedness and to participate in her judgment, the judgment appropriate for her adultery. She would be stripped of clothing and possessions, left vulnerable and exposed before the swords and stones which would bring about her shameful destruction.

## Sinful Sisters (Ezekiel 16:44-59)

In this section, Ezekiel was led to describe further the wickedness of Jerusalem. That city was compared to two "sister-cities," Samaria and Sodom, renowned for their wickedness. Both cities had already been destroyed because of their ungodliness, and Jerusalem was quickly approaching the same fate. We have already studied the similarities between Jerusalem and Samaria, but what did Jerusalem have in common with Sodom? Interestingly the homosexual sin so well-known there was not mentioned, but instead the sins that gave birth to that sort of perverse indulgence were highlighted. They were these: *"pride, fullness of food, and abundance of idleness; neither did she strengthen the hand of the poor and needy"* (Ezekiel 16:49). Which, if not all of these, could apply to our own city or nation? Such sins led to the complete downfall of Jerusalem. Will our citizenry, guilty of the same things, be exempted much longer from God's judgment?

## Restored Covenant (Ezekiel 16:60-63)

Amazingly, right after this pledge of certain judgment, God renewed His promise to keep the covenant He had made with His people. At some future time, He would restore Jerusalem and re-establish His covenant with Israel, even bringing Samaria and Sodom back for them to watch over as daughters, an unexpected act of mercy. However, when such an undeserved atonement was provided for them by God, allowing them to come back to Him, they would be ashamed and speechless at the wonder of it. God forgives sin as we confess it. God remembers and keeps His covenant with those who love Him in any age, yet an awareness of our past sins should always keep us humble before Him and silent to any claim that we deserved any of it on our own.

## A Riddle and a Parable (Ezekiel 17)

Ezekiel had received the first vision he had recorded in this book in the fifth year of King Jehoiachin's captivity in Babylon (Ezekiel 1:2). Jehoiachin had followed in the steps of his wicked father Jehoiakim but only reigned three months in Jerusalem before the forces of Nebuchadnezzar came down and besieged the city, subsequently capturing Jehoiachin and many others and taking them off to Babylon (2 Kings 24:15,16). Nebuchadnezzar was the *"great eagle...full of feathers of various colors"* (Ezekiel 17:3), and Jehoiachin was the *"topmost young twig"* of the cedar of Lebanon which Nebuchadnezzar carried back to his land. The seed from that plant (Ezekiel 17:5) which he planted in a fertile field, allowing it to grow low but abundantly, was Zedekiah, Jehoiachin's uncle. Instead of being content with his **subservient** yet still prosperous position under the authority of Nebuchadnezzar, Zedekiah acted treacherously, spreading out his "roots" toward Egypt. Zedekiah, Ezekiel prophesied, would suffer for breaking his covenant with Nebuchadnezzar, and Egypt would not even move to help him. Zedekiah would be caught and taken back to Babylon, and instead of being allowed to exist as Nebuchadnezzar had first planned, Jerusalem would be destroyed. The fulfillment of this was just as Ezekiel prophesied and was recorded in 2 Kings 24:17 and following.

As the sickeningly vivid description of Jerusalem's condition in Chapter 16 was followed by a promise of her future redemption, so here the prophecy of the destruction of Jerusalem and the captivity of the last king of Judah was followed by one more promise of hope. God had Ezekiel announce that despite the efforts of Nebuchadnezzar to cut off the throne of David, God would preserve it. He Himself would take *"one of the highest branches of the high cedar and set it out."* God further promised, *"I will crop off from the topmost of its young twigs a tender one, and will plant it on a high and prominent mountain"* (Ezekiel 17:22). Keeping the same interpretation of the earlier riddle or parable, this means that God will preserve an heir to the line of David and will one day exalt that heir as the most majestic ruler of all. This promise was repeated through other prophets like Isaiah and Zechariah, who actually called this honored ruler *"the Branch"* (Isaiah 4:2 and Zechariah 3:8). Christians see its fulfillment in the Second Coming of Jesus to take the throne of David in the Millennial Kingdom. In Jesus, His Branch, God exalted *"the low tree, dried up the green tree and made the dry tree flourish"* (Ezekiel 17:24). Isaiah described this, too: *"For He shall grow up before Him as a tender plant, and as a root out of dry ground. He has no form or comeliness; and when we see Him, there is no beauty that we should desire Him"* (Isaiah 53:2).

## Corrective Thinking (Ezekiel 18)

As God exposed the idolatry in the hearts of the elders in Chapter 14, He here addressed another hidden problem: wrong thinking. As with idolatry or wrong focus, wrong thinking will also eventually become wrong acting. God wanted to stop any more of that. A popular but invalid proverb of Ezekiel's day was *"The fathers have eaten sour grapes, and the children's teeth are set on edge."* (Jeremiah commented on this same thing in Jeremiah 31:29,30.) This meant that children suffered from the things their parents chose to do, which at some level, was quite true. Children do suffer as a result of the evil actions of those in authority over them as the Second Commandment stated in its ban on idol-making: *"You shall not make for yourself a carved image...For I, the LORD your God, am a jealous God, visiting the iniquity of the fathers upon the children to the third and fourth generations of those who hate Me, but showing mercy to thousands, to those who love Me and keep My commandments"* (Exodus 20:4-6). However, thinking that what parents had done made the children helpless and hopeless victims without choices was not true. God wanted them to get away from this **fatalistic** attitude that kept them prisoners to the past and move away from evil to embrace the righteous will of God as their own.

God gave three scenarios to illustrate how His justice operated (Ezekiel 18:5-18). They all explained that a person was accountable to God for His own choices, not the choices of another, even one as close as a parent. God desired men to turn from their sin; He took no pleasure in handing down judgments on evil (Ezekiel 18:23). God went further to explain quite adamantly that He also expected righteous living to be continual and consistent. If a formerly righteous man turned to sin, he could expect sure and certain judgment if he did not repent. The writer of Hebrews repeated a similar warning to his readers:

*For if we sin willfully after we have received the knowledge of the truth, there no longer remains a sacrifice for sins, but a certain fearful expectation of judgment, and fiery indignation which will devour the adversaries. Anyone who has rejected Moses' law dies without mercy on the testimony of two or three witnesses. Of how much worse punishment, do you suppose, will he be thought worthy who has trampled the Son of God underfoot, counted the blood of the covenant by which he was sanctified a common thing, and insulted the Spirit of grace?* (Hebrews 10:26-29).

The chapter ended with a plea for repentance, a call to heed the warning to flee from the wrath to come. What were they to do? God was specific:

*"Cast away from you all the transgressions which you have committed, and get yourselves a new heart and a new spirit. For why should you die, O house of Israel? For I have no pleasure in the death of one who dies," says the Lord God. "Therefore turn and live!"* (Ezekiel 18:31,32).

## Lamentation over Jerusalem (Ezekiel 19)

The final chapter in this week's lesson is a lament or song of mourning over the certain fall of Jerusalem. The last of the line of David's descendants to rule over the nation would soon be taken to Babylon, thus ending further opportunity to rule. Judah's kings had shared a grand lineage. Like clever cubs of a proud lioness they started out well, but a recent one, Jehoahaz son of Josiah, had done evil in God's sight and had been captured by the pharaoh of Egypt and abruptly dethroned and taken to Egypt (Ezekiel 19:4; 2 Kings 23:31-33). Later, another "cub," a brother of Jehoahaz's named Zedekiah, would become the last king of Judah, but he, too, would make enemies and be captured, dethroned, and taken captive to Babylon (Ezekiel 19:9; 2 Kings 25:7).

Changing images, Ezekiel continued the lament. Judah had been a prized and **prolific** vine, producing strong branches for the making of many **scepters,** implying the production of many kings. However, from her high position, this choice vine was pulled down, dried up, broken apart, and consumed by fire. Planted now only in a wilderness, she seemed no longer to have any branch strong enough to produce another scepter. This certainly was a song of gloom and doom, appropriate for the coming funeral of a nation.

## Lessons This Week: Summarizing the Truths Presented

**EZEKIEL 14:** We cannot sin in secret. Our omniscient Father sees right into our very hearts. Idols in our hearts must be cast out. We must turn to Him and repent. Even the high-profile righteousness of those like Noah, Daniel, and Job cannot save us. We must be individually right with our Father.

**EZEKIEL 15:** He is the vine; we are the branches. Cut off from Him, we can produce nothing of value and can only expect the fire of His judgment.

**EZEKIEL 16:** The very blessings of God that make it possible for us not only to live but also to succeed and prosper might also become stumblingblocks to our righteous development. We must constantly remember the source of our blessings, the One who saw us filthy and abandoned and brought us into His family. Remembering keeps us humble and thankful and free from the poisons of pride.

**EZEKIEL 17:** Failure to submit to the discipline of the Lord brings worse restrictions and penalties. Zedekiah found that out the hard way. It appeared that the line of David in the kings of Judah would die with him, but God made a promise to plant a Righteous Branch and one day restore the throne to another heir.

**EZEKIEL 18:** Every individual has a responsibility to God to choose His righteousness consistently and continually. We are not helpless victims of our past. We can still choose to be *"more than conquerors"* through Christ. We must come to God and receive a new heart and a new Spirit that we might at last become able to serve Him as He deserves.

**EZEKIEL 19:** Judah faced her own funeral, and Ezekiel was already mourning her destruction. However, with our God, there is always the hope that He will turn our mourning into dancing and our sackcloth into gladness (Psalm 30:11). Even Christians face consequences of past sins, but not as those who have no hope. For the righteous, the funeral will be followed by a resurrection!

---

### VOCABULARY

1. **fatalistic:** believing that things are determined by fate and cannot be altered by personal action
2. **prolific:** growing or producing in great abundance or with great speed
3. **scepters:** rods or staffs carried by kings as a sign of authority
4. **subservient:** serving under the authority of another

# Notes

# Notes

# PROPHETS OF ISRAEL — LESSON 12

## Daily Bible Study Questions

**Study Procedure:** Read the Scripture references before answering questions. Unless otherwise instructed, use the Bible only in answering questions. Some questions may be more difficult than others but try to answer as many as you can. Pray for God's wisdom and understanding as you study and don't be discouraged if some answers are not obvious at first.

### THIS WEEK'S MEMORY VERSE:

(Ezekiel 22:30) *"So I sought for a man among them who would make a wall, and stand in the gap before Me on behalf of the land, that I should not destroy it; but I found no one."*

### FIRST DAY: Review of Ezekiel 14-19; Read Ezekiel 20:1-32

1. Matching:
   (a) Idols in our _____ must be cast out.
   (b) Even the high-profile righteousness of _____ cannot save us.
   (c) God is the _____; we are the _____.
   (d) Cut off from Him through disobedience we can produce _____ and only expect the _____ of His judgment.
   (e) By _____ what God has done we can be kept humble and thankful and free from the poisons of pride.
   (f) Though Babylon, with the capture and exile of King Zedekiah, seemed to cut down the majestic cedar representing the line of Judah, God promised to restore and magnify a _____.
   (g) We cannot please God in our own strength. He wants each person to come to Him to receive a new _____ and a new _____.
   (h) Judah faced her own _____, but God promised a future _____.

   1. heart, spirit
   2. vine, branches
   3. remembering
   4. funeral, resurrection
   5. Noah, Job, and Daniel
   6. Righteous Branch
   7. hearts
   8. nothing, fire

2. What did you learn or of what were you reminded in last week's lesson that was particularly meaningful?

# LESSON 12                                                    PROPHETS OF ISRAEL

3. Read Ezekiel 20:1-3. In the seventh year of their captivity (August 14, 591 B.C.), the elders of Israel came to Ezekiel to hear a fresh word from God. How did God respond to them?

4. Read Ezekiel 20:4-32. As an explanation for this, God told Ezekiel to give the elders a history lesson. What all were they doing, which their ancestors had done, that would bring to them the judgment their ancestors had received?

**SECOND DAY: Read Ezekiel 20:33-21:23**

5. Read Ezekiel 20:33-44. God's eternal covenant with Israel prevented Him from utterly destroying the people as they deserved, but what did He promise to do when He regathered them one final time at some point in the future?

6. Read Ezekiel 20:45-49.
   (a) What vision of judgment did Ezekiel record here?

   (b) What was the response of his listeners?

7. Read Ezekiel 21:1-7. Ezekiel was told to announce that the sword of the Lord was going to fall in judgment on Israel from south to north.
   (a) With what attitude or emotions was Ezekiel to make this announcement?

   (b) Why do you think God commanded that?

8. Read Ezekiel 21:8-17 which is a song or poem about God's chosen sword of judgment. What does it mean when it speaks about the sword's power over the scepter in verses 10 and 13?

Page 14

# LESSON 12
## PROPHETS OF ISRAEL

9. Read Ezekiel 21:18-24. Ezekiel was to put up signs at a place where the road from Babylon divided into two parts.
   (a) One sign pointed to _____.
   (b) One sign pointed to _____.
   (c) The king of Babylon's use of occult rituals would lead him to choose to go to _____.

**THIRD DAY: Continue in Ezekiel 21; Read Ezekiel 22**

10. Read Ezekiel 21:25-27 for Ezekiel's prophetic comments to the *"wicked prince of Israel"* (that is, King Zedekiah - see 2 Kings 25:2-7) at the time of Babylon's final attack. What phrase indicated that another king would one day arise to continue the line that seemed to be ending with Zedekiah?

11. Read Ezekiel 21:28-32. How complete a judgment would soon fall on the Ammonites?

12. Read Ezekiel 22. Write the number of the verse(s) in which the following descriptions of these sins of Jerusalem are found.
    _____ (a) bloodshed
    _____ (b) idolatry
    _____ (c) dishonoring of parents
    _____ (d) oppression of strangers
    _____ (e) mistreatment of widows and orphans
    _____ (f) sexual sin
    _____ (g) bribery and usury
    _____ (h) breaking the Sabbath
    _____ (i) failure to "stand in the gap" for God and pray for the land

**FOURTH DAY: Read Ezekiel 23**

13. Read Ezekiel 23:1-4. In this graphic allegory about two promiscuous sisters, Oholah was the name given for _____ and Oholibah was the name given for _____. (**Note:** Oholah meant "her own tabernacle"—an allusion to the man-made religious idolatry of the northern kingdom, while Oholibah meant "My tabernacle is in her"—an allusion to the Lord's temple centered there.)

14. Read Ezekiel 23:5-10. With whom did Oholah make an inappropriate alliance and with what result?

15. Read Ezekiel 23:11-21. Oholibah had not learned from the mistakes of her sister. With whom did she corrupt herself instead of staying faithful to God?

Page 15

# LESSON 12   PROPHETS OF ISRAEL

16. What was going to happen to Oholibah? (Ezekiel 23:22-49)

17. What were some of the more shocking sins committed in Jerusalem?

**FIFTH DAY:  Read Ezekiel 24**

18. Read Ezekiel 24:1-14. Even though Ezekiel was in Babylon, weeks away from receiving any fresh news from Jerusalem, God informed him, through the Holy Spirit, that on the tenth day of the tenth month of the ninth year of their captivity (January 15, 588 B.C.), the Babylonian siege against Jerusalem would begin. What do you think the "cooking pot demonstration" was supposed to illustrate to Ezekiel's audience about what was happening in the *"bloody city"* of Jerusalem?

19. Read Ezekiel 24:15-18. This must have been Ezekiel's most difficult "living parable."
    (a) What happened to Ezekiel?

    (b) How did God tell him to respond?

20. Read Ezekiel 24:19-27. What was this to signify to Ezekiel's fellow captives?

21. What would happen to confirm what God had supernaturally revealed to Ezekiel? (See also Ezekiel 33:21,22 and Ezekiel 3:26,27.)

22. God revealed things to Ezekiel, who, along with his fellow captives, was being spared from the brutal Babylonian siege of Jerusalem. Why do you think God wanted Ezekiel to record and report God's explanation of what was happening in Jerusalem?

# Ezekiel 20-24

## The Righteousness of God's Judgment on Israel (Ezekiel 20:1-32)

On August 14, 591 B.C., in the seventh year of captivity, the elders of the exile appealed to Ezekiel for a fresh word from God. Before they could even formulate their questions, God told Ezekiel to tell them that He would not entertain any more inquiries from them. Blinded to their own sin, they would only be allowed to hear how they had become just like their idolatrous ancestors and therefore deserving of their present **predicament** and future judgment. To prove this, Ezekiel reviewed Israel's past, starting with her exile in Egypt.

At that time God had graciously revealed Himself to the huge family of Jacob, now a nation in themselves, carefully instructing them to throw away the idols of Egypt and worship Him alone as their one true God (Ezekiel 20:7). However, they did not obey Him in this, and He almost destroyed them before they even got out of Egypt (Ezekiel 20:8). Only for the sake of His own Name (because the Egyptians would have misunderstood any other response on His part as an inability to save His people), God went ahead and delivered them from Egypt anyway and took them into the wilderness. There He gave them further teaching, revealing His commandments in written form and instructing them about observing a Sabbath, which would make them distinct among the other nations and serve as a covenant sign of their loyalty to God.

But they soon broke His clear commandments and refused to observe the Sabbath; right there in the wilderness, God almost destroyed Israel again. However, for His own Name's sake, lest the Gentiles misunderstand His power, He did not destroy them at once. He let the older generation die-off over a period of forty years, only allowing their children to enter the land of promise. Characteristically, the generations following also disobeyed God's statutes, profaned His Sabbaths, and returned to idolatry—even sacrificing their children to pagan idols. God's response then was to withdraw His hand from them, leaving them to continue in their sins, but vowing to *"scatter them among the Gentiles and disperse them throughout the countries"* (Ezekiel 20:23).

As before, in defense of His Name and reputation among the Gentiles, God could not allow His covenant people to carry on "business as usual" while disobeying every command He had given to make them distinct among the heathen and to lead them toward holiness. G. Campbell Morgan explained that for God to permit "that people to remain a nation among the nations, would have been to perpetuate a misrepresentation of God among those nations" (*Life Applications from Every Chapter of the Bible,* p. 263). For His Name's sake, He had to remove Israel from the place He had given her.

## Sabbath Breaking

Did you notice the repetition of the mention of Sabbath-breaking in each generation as one of the reasons God was displeased with Israel? The stopping of regular work and the participating in public worship one day a week was a command God had given them that had at least a threefold purpose: (1) It would bring needed rest to them, their servants, and animals and the break in routine would rejuvenate them physically for the week that followed. (2) Observing the Sabbath would give them the opportunity to lead their families in right worship as well as assemble in public groups for religious instruction. This would refresh them spiritually. (3) Honoring the Sabbath would make them distinct from the other people-groups around them, revealing the freedom God had won for them to set their own schedules.

What do our Sunday practices do for us physically, spiritually, and in the area of public witness? The command to live differently and intentionally one day out of seven was given at Creation and has never been revoked. Is this an area of your life which you need to reevaluate?

## Future Return of Exiles (Ezekiel 20:33-44)

Even though God had to remove His people from their place because of the terrible witness to His covenant purposes they were giving to the nations around them, He promised, in this section, to bring them back one day from their exile and rule over them with *"a mighty hand, with an outstretched arm, and with fury poured out"* (Ezekiel 20:33). Like the exodus from Egypt, in which the rebels died in the wilderness before the next generation could enter Canaan, God would one day bring His people out from all the places He had scattered them, **purging** any remaining rebels before allowing the proven righteous to re-enter Jerusalem. That selected group would finally honor Him before the Gentiles, remembering and repenting of their earlier rebellion against His commands. This final regathering of the Jews was similarly described in Ezekiel 11:17-20 as well as in Zechariah 8:1-17.

## Coming Judgment on the Land of Israel (Ezekiel 20:45-49)

Ezekiel was told in this passage to again set his face against Israel. He was to prophesy that from the forest lands of the South on northward God would start a fire to scorch the whole land in judgment for their sins. Ezekiel's audience, probably unable to bear such news, accused him of not speaking plainly. This distressed him, but he was just God's messenger, unable to make them believe.

## The Sword Sent by God (Ezekiel 21:1-17)

In further explanation of the coming fire of judgment on the whole geographical area called Israel, God had Ezekiel speak poetically of the sword of the Lord now unsheathed. Sharpened and polished, Ezekiel announced in great grief, the sword of the Lord would be put into the hand of Babylon to cut off even the scepter or right-to-rule of the king of Judah.

## Ezekiel's Marking of the Roadways (Ezekiel 21:18-27)

In another of his "living parables," Ezekiel obeyed God's orders to mark the road from Babylon, coming southwest, at the point where it forked near Israel. He was to make signs showing that one way led to Rabbah of Ammon and the other to Jerusalem in Judah. At that place the king of Babylon would stop and use **divination** and occult techniques to determine which way to go. He would be led to go to Jerusalem, though the Jews there would think it was all a terrible mistake. It would not be a mistake. God would allow Babylon to be His punishing sword, bringing judgment on all the sins of His people, especially those of the *"profane, wicked prince of Israel,"* Zedekiah. In a poem or song, Ezekiel called for Zedekiah to remove his turban and crown in anticipation of his coming humiliation. His throne, which was the throne of David, would be cast down *"until He comes whose right it is, and [God] will give it to Him"* (Ezekiel 21:27). This was a prophecy of the Second Coming of Israel's Messiah, Jesus Christ. In the meantime, though, there would be no descendant of David's to reign over Israel.

## Ammon Threatened, Too (Ezekiel 21:28-32)

Israel's old enemy Ammon would be threatened by the drawn sword of Babylon, too, but that sword would be returned to its sheath. One day God Himself would judge Ammon with no promise given that He would ever restore it. In fact, He promised, when He had finished with them, they would not even be remembered (Ezekiel 21:32).

## The Bloody City (Ezekiel 22)

Still defending God's righteousness in judging Jerusalem, Ezekiel recorded the catalogue of sins God had revealed to him which were being actively promoted in that bloody city: murder, idolatry, political corruption, dishonoring of parents, oppression of strangers, mistreatment of widows and orphans, Sabbath-breaking, sexual perversions of all kinds, bribery, and extortion (Ezekiel 22:1-16). Like a metal-worker, God would place them over the fires of His wrath to salvage any usable metals from the **dross,** but they were all dross (Ezekiel 22:17-22)!

Not only was the general population indulging in lawlessness, but also the entire Jewish leadership. Prophets, priests, and princes failed to distinguish between the holy and the unholy. God declared: *"So I sought for a man among them who would make a wall, and stand in the gap before Me on behalf of the land, that I should not destroy it; but I found no one"* (Ezekiel 22:30). So in the absence of a single **intercessor** or mediator, God went forward with His judgment.

## Tale of Two Sister-Cities (Ezekiel 23)

In an allegorical poem, Ezekiel described the sinful actions and resulting judgment on the sister-cities of Jerusalem and Samaria. The name given in the **allegory** to Samaria was Oholah, meaning "her own tabernacle." This was probably an allusion to the fact that many in the Northern Kingdom had refused to worship properly at God's "tabernacle" or temple in Jerusalem and had invented their own way of worship, making use of golden calves placed in worship centers within their own boundaries. Jerusalem was called Oholibah which meant "My tabernacle is in her." Jerusalem had had the advantage of being home first to the tabernacle (later the temple of God), the site God had designated as the only proper place for worship.

Oholah (Samaria) was described as having lusted after other lovers, breaking covenant with the Lord, her Husband. However, her alliance with Assyria backfired and she was attacked and conquered by that nation. Oholibah (Jerusalem) had not learned from her sister's mistakes over a century before. She had lusted after not only Assyria, but also Egypt and Babylon, and she, too, would subsequently be conquered and captured by her last "lover."

God's righteous pronouncement in Ezekiel 23:35 explained their fall: *"Because you have forgotten Me and cast Me behind your back, therefore you shall bear the penalty of your lewdness and your harlotry."* How bad were they? The people of Jerusalem not only killed their own children to make offerings to idols but also went into God's temple on the same day! Their shocking and sickening ways of worship had to be stopped, and God would do it quickly, convincing them at last—but too late to save them—of His right to rule the world (Ezekiel 23:49).

## The Lesson of the Cooking Pot (Ezekiel 24:1-14)

On the very same day that the Babylonian siege began in Jerusalem, Ezekiel was told to record the date and *"utter a parable to the rebellious house"* of Israel. He told them to put on a pot, filling it with every good piece of meat they could find. The pot would symbolize Jerusalem, the meat represented the remaining inhabitants, and the fire under it, igniting piles of bones, pictured Babylon. The contents would serve no good purpose; the fire would only bring to the top the deep scum forming inside. The fire would burn till the contents was consumed and then keep burning till the pot was cleansed of its filthiness. Jerusalem's judgment would be total.

What caused God to send this fire of judgment on Jerusalem? It was mainly her long-time disregard for the sanctity of human life: *"For her blood is in her midst; she set it on top of a rock; she did not pour it on the ground, to cover it with dust. That it may raise up fury and take vengeance, I have set her blood on top of a rock, that it may not be covered...Woe to the bloody city!"* (Ezekiel 24:7-9).

## The Removal of "The Desire of Your Eyes" (Ezekiel 24:15-27)

In one last startling action to get the attention of the exiles, God told Ezekiel that He would strike Ezekiel's wife suddenly with death. However, Ezekiel was only to mourn inwardly and privately; he was not to use any of the traditional rites commonly employed in public mourning. That evening, his wife did die, and the next morning Ezekiel carried on as God had commanded. As God knew they would, the people questioned this strange reaction, giving Ezekiel the opportunity to prophesy their future sorrow. Soon they, too, would lose the desire of their eyes, when Jerusalem fell and the temple was destroyed. Like Ezekiel, they would not mourn publicly either. These words of prophecy would soon be confirmed, God said, when an escapee from the siege at Jerusalem made his way to them to announce the tragedy. (See Ezekiel 33:21.) As a sign, on that day Ezekiel would be healed of the muteness God had earlier put on him (Ezekiel 3:26) and be free to answer their questions.

## Reviewing Ezekiel's Defense of God's Right to Judge Israel

In this week's lesson, Ezekiel defended the righteousness of God's decision to judge Israel. He chronicled her people's continuous participation in sin by reviewing their past, exposing their present, and foretelling their future. Jerusalem, the jewel of the nations and the selected site for God's own temple, had become a city of bloody corruption. Her existence dishonored His Name, and the fires of judgment had to be employed to cleanse her. Not only would the city fall but also the kingdom. Judah's last king would be captured and the line of Judah suspended until some time in the distant future when the true and righteous Heir of David would return to rule. Scattered among the nations would be the remnant of God's covenant people, but not forever. God promised to regather them finally and purge them one more time, allowing those who truly loved Him to inhabit again the place He had prepared for them. In seventy years this would be partially fulfilled, but the complete fulfillment would wait until the return of Christ.

God's discipline of His people today is always in line with His righteousness, too. We are not to question the rightness of His judgments but to seek the causes for them. Complete, quick, and heartfelt confession of sin can turn off some of the heat beneath the cauldron of our lives, personally and nationally. Will we learn from Israel's history or just repeat it? Each generation has to decide anew.

### VOCABULARY

1. **allegory:** the expression by means of symbolic fictional figures and actions of truths or generalizations about human existence
2. **divination:** the occultic practice of divining the will of the gods by drawing lots, examining the entrails of animals, discerning signs in the heavens, or other means
3. **dross:** an impurity that forms on the surface of molten metal
4. **intercessor:** one who entreats or prays on behalf of others
5. **predicament:** troubling, puzzling, or difficult situation
6. **purging:** making clean, freeing from guilt or sin

# Notes

# Notes

# PROPHETS OF ISRAEL — LESSON 13

## Daily Bible Study Questions

**Study Procedure:** Read the Scripture references before answering questions. Unless otherwise instructed, use the Bible only in answering questions. Some questions may be more difficult than others but try to answer as many as you can. Pray for God's wisdom and understanding as you study and don't be discouraged if some answers are not obvious at first.

**THIS WEEK'S MEMORY VERSE:**

(Ezekiel 28:15) *"You were perfect in your ways from the day you were created, till iniquity was found in you."*

**FIRST DAY: Review of Ezekiel 20-24; Circle the best answers**

1. In the review of the history of Israel given in Ezekiel 20, which of these sins were repeated by every generation of that nation?
   (a) idolatry    (b) Sabbath-breaking    (c) neglect of commandments
   (d) child-sacrifice    (e) gambling    (f) gossip

2. The *"sword of the Lord"* chosen to destroy Judah, according to Ezekiel 21, was
   (a) Ammon    (b) Edom    (c) Assyria    (d) Babylon    (e) Egypt

3. In Ezekiel 22 when God, like a metal worker, put the fire to the cauldron of Jerusalem, what was the result?
   (a) silver    (b) bronze    (c) iron    (d) lead    (e) dross

4. The two harlot sisters described in the allegory of Chapter 23 were whom?
   (a) Judah    (b) Israel    (c) Jerusalem    (d) Samaria    (e) Nineveh

5. In what very difficult "living parable" did Ezekiel participate in Chapter 24?
   (a) the fall of Jerusalem
   (b) the sudden death of his wife
   (c) a new exile to Assyria

**SECOND DAY: Read Ezekiel 25, 26, 27**

6. In Ezekiel 25, God told Ezekiel to proclaim several judgments on countries surrounding Israel. Match the crimes to the guilty countries. (Consult a map to see their proximity to Judah.)

   _____(a) Ammon
   _____(b) Moab
   _____(c) Edom
   _____(d) Philistia

   1. They *"took vengeance with a spiteful heart, to destroy because of an old hatred."*
   2. They denied God's power and said, *"Look! The house of Judah is like all the nations."*
   3. They laughed and mocked when the sanctuary was destroyed, the land was made desolate, and the people of Judah went into captivity.
   4. They took vengeance on Judah, which greatly offended God.

# LESSON 13
## PROPHETS OF ISRAEL

7. Read Ezekiel 26. List three or four specific things that would happen to Tyre for their lack of compassion for Jerusalem when she was conquered by Nebuchadnezzar.

8. Read Ezekiel 27. The fall of Tyre would be seen as tragic by those who enjoyed a rich trade with her. List some of the types of merchandise in which she traded.

## THIRD DAY: Read Ezekiel 28:1-19 and Isaiah 14:12-17

9. The prince of Tyre, during the time of Nebuchadnezzar's last attack on Jerusalem, seemed to be quite arrogant.
   (a) What claims did he make for himself?

   (b) For what talents or achievements did the Lord give him credit? (Ezekiel 28:1-5)

   (c) What did God plan to do to humble him? (Ezekiel 28:6-10)

10. With verse eleven, the Holy Spirit had Ezekiel change from speaking of the prince of Tyre to speaking of the king of Tyre. Over the centuries, many Bible scholars have seen Ezekiel's lament over the king of Tyre as a sort of revelation, or pulling back of the curtain, to expose the dark influence behind the prince of Tyre's egotistical actions. In this view, verses 11-19 are accepted as a description of the origin and history of Satan.
    (a) What did he look like?

    (b) To what places did he have access?

    (c) What were his talents?

    (d) What was his position, title, or angelic classification?

Page 24

# LESSON 13            PROPHETS OF ISRAEL

    (e) What was God's assessment of him?

    (f) What caused his downfall?

    (g) What was his final state?

11. Read Isaiah 14:12-17 for the passage which began with a prophecy about the king of Babylon but continued with what has been accepted by many as another description of Satan. What details are found in this passage about Satan that were not included in Ezekiel's description.

## FOURTH DAY: Read Ezekiel 28:20-30:26

12. Read Ezekiel 28:20-26. For what purpose was God executing judgment on Sidon and the rest of the nations surrounding Israel?

13. In Chapter 29 Pharaoh, king of Egypt, was to be judged for two main sins. What were they?
    (a) verses 3-5

    (b) verses 6,7

14. Seventeen years later, Ezekiel received another prophecy about Egypt. Read Ezekiel 29:8-21.
    (a) What would the judgment on Egypt include?

    (b) How long would it last?

    (c) What country would be used to accomplish it?

15. Read Ezekiel 30. Give a few further details from this chapter about the judgment on Egypt that were not in the previous chapter.

**FIFTH DAY: Read Ezekiel 31 and 32**
16. Read Ezekiel 31.
    (a) What imagery did Ezekiel use to describe the greatness of Assyria? (Ezekiel 31:1-9)

    (b) Did that kingdom endure? Explain. (Ezekiel 31:10-17)

    (c) Would Egypt keep her high position in the world? Explain. (Ezekiel 31:18)

17. Ezekiel 32 is a lament or funeral speech about the fall of Pharaoh and his kingdom in Egypt.
    (a) To what is he compared in Ezekiel 32:1,2?

    (b) List some of the poetic descriptions of Egypt's fall from Ezekiel 32:3-16.

18. Read Ezekiel 32:17-32. What nations were seen as being among those destined for Hell or the Pit?

19. What word did you find repeated over and over in the descriptions of this passage about those headed for hell, and what do you think it means in the context of this week's lesson?

# Notes

## EZEKIEL 25-32

### God's Judgment on Seven Neighboring Nations

In Ezekiel 25-32 are contained the prophecies of judgment on seven of Judah's neighboring nations. Each nation would be brought to judgment because of the way in which they had abused or failed to help God's people.

### Ammon (Ezekiel 25:1-7)

The Ammonites were related to Israel and Judah through their ancestor Ammon, the son of Lot, nephew of Abraham (Genesis 19:35-38). However, as a nation, they had a history of showing **antagonism** toward their kinsmen. (See Judges 10:8; 11:11-33; 1 Samuel 11:1-11; 2 Samuel 10 and 11; 2 Chronicles 20:1-23; 27:5; Jeremiah 40:14; 49:1; and Nehemiah 4:7.) The judgment Ezekiel pronounced was brought on by their celebration of the destruction of Jerusalem and the captivity of her inhabitants. Performed from their good-viewing position just east of Judah, across the Jordan River, their celebration "dance" (note the use of hand-clapping and foot-stamping in verse 6) was especially inappropriate since they had just missed being attacked by Babylon themselves (Ezekiel 21:18-23). God said He would bring on them the very thing they had rejoiced over happening to His people—plunder and destruction. We should note that it is still quite dangerous to oppose that which God has had His hand upon. Remember David's unwillingness to kill the deranged Saul, leaving judgment completely to God, because he recognized that Saul was nevertheless *"the Lord's anointed"* (1 Samuel 26:9-11)?

### Moab (Ezekiel 25:8-11)

The original Moab was a man, who like Ammon, had been the son of Lot, the nephew of Abraham. That made Moab's descendants kinsmen of Israel, too, and like the Ammonites, the Moabites had been antagonists of Israel for generations. (For examples of their long-time opposition see Deuteronomy 2:9, Judges 11:17, Joshua 24:9, and 2 Kings 24:2). When Jerusalem fell after the terrible siege enforced by Babylon, the Moabites claimed, *"Look! The house of Judah is like all the nations"* (Ezekiel 25:8). The meaning of this was that they believed Judah's claim to be false—the claim of being the distinctive people of God. Obviously, to the Moabites, the God of Judah was no better than the gods of Moab since He had apparently been unable to protect His people. This, of course, was blasphemy, and God would judge it by letting Moab, right along with Ammon, be taken over by forces from the East. God would bring a final end to their cruelties against Judah and the **maligning** of His good name.

### Edom (Ezekiel 25:12-14)

The Edomites had not just laughed at the fall of Jerusalem or mocked the God of Israel as had Ammon and Moab, they had also actively fought against God's people. So God announced He would now fight against them, too. Amos, Obadiah, and Jeremiah had already prophesied the fall of Edom, and God used Ezekiel to give further confirmation of their words.

### Philistia (Ezekiel 25:15-17)

God was judging Philistia because of her vengeance on His people which had been carried out *"with a spiteful heart,"* enflamed by an *"old hatred."* Though the Philistines did not at that time recognize God as Lord of all, they soon would when He released His vengeance on them (Ezekiel 25:17). G. Campbell Morgan, an Anglican theologian, provided this insight into God's judgment of these nations: "Here is the one purpose of Jehovah in His dealings with all nations. Those who fail to find Him in the light of His revelation of Himself by law or in the natural order, He brings to know Him through judgment" (*Life Applications from Every Chapter in the Bible,* p. 265).

### Tyre (Ezekiel 26)

A little more than a year after the fall of Jerusalem, Ezekiel was inspired to speak this series of prophecies against Tyre, a one-time ally of Judah's. Tyre's reaction to the fall of Jerusalem had been one of joy; after all, a big rival to her vast commercial enterprises and an obstacle to an open trade-route to Africa had been removed. Judah's loss, so Tyre thought, would be her gain (Ezekiel 26:2).

Three chapters were devoted to the condemnation of Tyre, so big an enemy she was in God's eyes. In this chapter the destruction of the city was described. Tyre was actually a divided city, half on the northern coast of the Mediterranean sea and the other part a half-mile out from shore on an island. Tyre carried on much of its trade by way of the Mediterranean Sea, so the sea-side and island parts of its city were quite useful. Tyre also had some outlying suburbs or "daughter villages" where farming occurred (Ezekiel 26:6). Ezekiel explained that these were also going to be targets for God's judgment.

Ezekiel announced that Babylon would be recruited again to administer God's vengeance on Tyre. They would use battering rams to destroy the walls and axes to break down the towers. Tyre's conquerors would not only destroy the city but they would also throw the debris into the water, leaving the city "scraped" and bare like the top of a rock.

Babylon kept up a thirteen-year siege of Tyre (585-572 B.C.) and destroyed the city's holdings on the mainland. However, the city on the island was not destroyed until 332 B.C. At that time Alexander the Great besieged it for seven months and then used the debris from the island-city's destruction to build a causeway connecting the island to the city on the coast. This failure on Babylon's part to utterly destroy Tyre and profit from her wealth was the subject of another prophesy in Ezekiel 29:17. God gave Babylon the wealth of Egypt to make up for what had been left in Tyre's island-city. How amazing is the exact fulfillment of God's word!

## Funeral Song for Tyre (Ezekiel 27)

Since the prophecies of God are always sure and certain, Ezekiel was inspired to compose the funeral song or lamentation ahead of time for the future burial of Tyre. Her destruction was compared to that of the sinking of a fine ship. An inventory of her costly parts was made, show-casing the far-off places into which she went to trade: planks from a famous mountain range known for cedars called Senir, a mast from Lebanon, oars from the oaks of Bashan, inlays on her planks by craftsmen of Ashur, ivory from Cyprus, fine linen from Egypt, and costly dyes from Elishah, a city thought to be on Cyprus. A further catalogue of customers and suppliers was given through the poetic allusions to her oarsmen, pilots, and men of war who were from Sidon and Arvad (cities of Phoenicia), Persia (Iran), Lydia (Asia Minor), and Libya (Northern Africa). The references continued with mention of areas known today as Turkey, Russia, Spain, Greece, and Arabia. Ezekiel's **eulogy** of Tyre provided the most complete list of trade-cities in the Scriptures. From west to east the cities were named, providing a travel-guide for the commercial activities of that day. The choice items listed among her merchandise spoke of a very wealthy clientele. All Tyre's described **opulence** made her destruction seem all the more tragic, and those who were alive to witness her destruction would weep bitterly and mourn publicly for the loss to their world's economy. The city itself, once proud and rich, would be hissed at and forgotten.

## The Prince of Tyre (Ezekiel 28:1-10)

Addressing the prince of Tyre, Ezekiel exposed his part in the fall of that city. The prince of Tyre was the recognized leader, and yet the vast commercial successes had made him proud and boastful, blind to the dangerous judgment God had ordained. He actually claimed to be a god, a possessor of great wisdom, and yet in the future when he was captured by strangers, slain, and sent to the Pit, he would realize he was just a mere man, sharing the fate of all the uncircumcised, those out of covenant with the true God.

## The King of Tyre (Ezekiel 28:11-19)

There are a variety of interpretations for this passage. Some see it as a rather grand allegory about the danger of pride in high places, while others treat it as a fanciful (but obviously contradictory) account of the fall of Adam. But one interesting view that seems to be more in keeping with the rest of Scripture and the context of the earlier part of the chapter, is that this is a description of the supernatural power who inspired the egotistical actions of the just-described prince of Tyre. The Holy Spirit gave this power or personage the title of "king" of Tyre, as if to indicate his superiority to the "prince" who was earlier described as ruling Tyre on earth. This view sees in these verses a concise biography of Satan. From it, the following information can be gleaned:

1. Satan was created wise and perfect in beauty, adorned with a covering of nine of the twelve jewels that later were to be included in the breastplate of Israel's high priest (Ezekiel 28:12,13).

2. His realm of influence or talent included instrumental music (Ezekiel 28:13).

3. He was an angel, of the order of cherub (which Ezekiel had mentioned in Chapter 10), who had been anointed to cover or protect the throne of God (Ezekiel 28:14).

4. He had access not only to the Garden of Eden but also to the holy mountain of God (Ezekiel 28:13,14; See also Job 1:6).

5. Success in trading made him violent; great beauty made him proud. For these sins, God cast him out of his appointed position, and one day would bring about his absolute destruction (Ezekiel 28:16-19).

(Note: A companion passage to this that also seems to speak of some evil personage beyond the human realm can be found in Isaiah 14. Refer to that for more information to complement Ezekiel's vision of this evil personality. Also see 1 Chronicles 21:1 for a reference to Satan's interest in the affairs of nations and Matthew 16:23 for an incident where Jesus turned to Peter but spoke directly to Satan.)

## Judgment on Sidon (Ezekiel 28:20-24)

Ezekiel proclaimed God's coming judgment on Sidon, a seaport north of Tyre. With Sidon's destruction, the last of Israel's nearest enemies would be gone, all of whom would certainly know by then that the God of Israel was real.

## Judgment on Egypt (Ezekiel 29)

Ezekiel's pronouncements on Egypt filled three chapters of his writings. The first message was written about seven months before the fall of Jerusalem and was dated January 7, 587 B.C. In it, Egypt was figuratively referred to as a great sea monster, lying in the midst of the famous Nile River. For making the arrogant claim of ownership and even creation of the Nile (Ezekiel 29:3), as well as for failing to keep its promises to Israel (Ezekiel 29:6,7), the great Egyptian monster would be caught, dragged ashore, and used as food for wild animals (Ezekiel 29:3-5). Then God promised to leave Egypt uninhabited for forty years, her inhabitants scattered among the nations. However, from their exile, God would bring them back to their land but would never allow them to regain their prominent position in world affairs (Ezekiel 29:12-16). In a second pronouncement, dated April 26, 571 B.C., (seventeen years after the prophecy given in Ezekiel 29:1), God had Ezekiel announce that Babylon would be His tool for judgment on Egypt (Ezekiel 29:17-20) and would receive the plunders from Egypt as its reward for being God's instrument of judgment against Tyre prior to this.

## Egypt and Her Allies (Ezekiel 30)

In this description of God's judgment on Egypt, Ezekiel announced that those nations with whom Egypt had been allied would also face His judgment in the near future (Ezekiel 30:5-19). Next, God had Ezekiel pronounce judgment on Egypt's leader, her pharaoh. God would break his power, figuratively his "arm," and leave him helpless against Babylon's forces, allowing them easy victory. This pronouncement, as did the others, finished with God's claim, *"Then they shall know that I am the LORD."*

## Egypt Cut Down (Ezekiel 31)

Comparing Egypt to the unexpectedly toppled Assyrian kingdom, Ezekiel revealed how foolish it was for Egypt to believe her people could escape God's hand of judgment. They were all headed to hell and needed to wake up to that eventuality.

## Lament over Pharaoh (Ezekiel 32:1-16)

On March 3, 585 B.C., Ezekiel delivered the fifth of his seven oracles against Egypt, all pronounced in a little over a two-year period. This one focused on the guilt of Egypt's leader, her pharaoh, in his nation's downfall. In God's net, this leader, like a proud lion or giant sea monster, would be caught and cast out in the open to be food for birds and beasts. God would mark the event with signs in the heavens, causing the hearts of many to be troubled. In a sixth pronouncement, beginning with verse 11, Ezekiel announced that for the judgment on Pharaoh and his land, God would again employ Babylon's mighty warriors. The land and waterways of Egypt would be left so empty of inhabitants that the rivers, no longer muddied by traffic, would flow clear.

## Hell: Destination of the Uncircumcised (Ezekiel 32:17-32)

On April 27, 586 B.C., God authorized Ezekiel to release the final pronouncement against Egypt, which was a description of hell, the place to which her inhabitants and allies were headed. What were some of the characteristics of hell described here?

1. The direction to it was downward; Ezekiel called it *"the Pit."*

2. It was inhabited by the uncircumcised. According to Genesis 17:10-14, circumcision was the sign of the covenant each Israelite male was to have made in his body by having the foreskin of his penis cut away when he was eight days old. It was the outward and visible sign of an inward and spiritual relationship with the true God who had redeemed him. Those outside God's covenant, collectively called the uncircumcised, were those who would be sentenced to hell.

3. The nationalities of the individual inhabitants were still recognizable, indicating that a person's individual characteristics will still be distinguishable in that place. Some in the Pit were Assyrians (Ezekiel 32:22); Elamites (from the area now known as Iraq - Ezekiel 32:24), residents of Meshech and Tubal (cities in Asia Minor - Ezekiel 32:26), Edomites (Ezekiel 32:29), and Sidonians (Ezekiel 32:30).

4. Misery loves company. Ezekiel wrote that upon recognizing the others, *"Pharaoh will see them and be comforted over all his multitude..."* (Ezekiel 32:31). The self-centeredness symptomatic of the uncircumcised will not be diminished in hell.

## Summing Up

While God offers mercy to any who will receive it (John 3:16), He promises judgment for those who refuse to acknowledge Him as Lord of all. While He chastises His own people for their sins in order to bring them back into obedience, He consigns those who hate Him—great and small—to hell forever. Ezekiel did not mince words in these prophecies. He made clear that, in regard to the Lord, only two positions are ever available: inside or outside of God's saving covenant. Where are you?

---

### VOCABULARY
1. **antagonism:** hostility, a condition of being against someone or something
2. **eulogy:** a speech that honors or praises someone, usually given at a funeral
3. **maligning:** speaking evil of someone, slandering
4. **opulence:** wealth in abundance

# Notes

# Notes

# PROPHETS OF ISRAEL — LESSON 14

## Daily Bible Study Questions

**Study Procedure:** Read the Scripture references before answering questions. Unless otherwise instructed, use the Bible only in answering questions. Some questions may be more difficult than others but try to answer as many as you can. Pray for God's wisdom and understanding as you study and don't be discouraged if some answers are not obvious at first.

### THIS WEEK'S MEMORY VERSE:

(Ezekiel 33:11) *"Say to them: 'As I live,' says the Lord GOD, 'I have no pleasure in the death of the wicked, but that the wicked turn from his way and live....'"*

### FIRST DAY: Review of Ezekiel 25-32; Read Ezekiel 33:1-20

1. There were some colorful descriptions given in Ezekiel's prophecies. Match the description to the person, place, or thing.

    _____(a) *"who was the gateway of the peoples"*

    _____(b) She was like a magnificent ship, but she would *"fall into the midst of the seas on the day of [her] ruin."*

    _____(c) *"Because your heart is lifted up, and you say, 'I am a god,'...."*

    _____(d) *"You were the anointed cherub who covers...."*

    _____(e) *"O great monster who lies in the midst of his rivers, who has said, 'My River is my own; I have made it for myself.'"*

    _____(f) *"a cedar in Lebanon, with fine branches that shaded the forest, and of high stature...."*

    _____(g) the destination of the uncircumcised, a place of shame

    1. Tyre
    2. King of Egypt
    3. Prince of Tyre
    4. The Pit
    5. Assyria
    6. Jerusalem
    7. King of Tyre

2. Describe briefly one or two things you learned about Satan or hell from last week's lesson.

3. Read Ezekiel 33:1-11. What is the responsibility of a watchman and what are the consequences of failing to carry it out?

4. Does God take pleasure in the death of the wicked? Support your answer with a verse.

# LESSON 14                                    PROPHETS OF ISRAEL

5. Read Ezekiel 33:12-20. In these verses God is defending the way He judges people. Why do you think some accuse Him of being unfair?

**SECOND DAY: Finish Ezekiel 33; Read Ezekiel 34**

6. Read Ezekiel 33:21-29. A survivor came to the exiles in Babylon to report on the fall of Jerusalem, but God went beyond that report to reveal to Ezekiel the inner thoughts of those who survived there. They mistakenly thought, having escaped the takeover of their city by Babylon, that they would now prosper, outdoing even Abraham. Summarize what God told Ezekiel to prophesy concerning them.

7. Read Ezekiel 33:30-33. Ezekiel was popular after all his prophecies about the fall of Jerusalem had been confirmed, but God warned him about those who were now praising him. What did God say about them?

8. Read Ezekiel 34:1-16. Using the commonly understood imagery of shepherd and sheep, God had Ezekiel contrast the failures of the past "shepherds" of Israel with the Lord's future efforts on Israel's behalf. Summarize some of the major contrasts below:

|  | With Israel's Past Shepherds | With Israel's Good Shepherd |
|---|---|---|
| (a) **What happened to the sheep?** | | |
| (b) **Where did the sheep dwell?** | | |

Page 34

# LESSON 14    PROPHETS OF ISRAEL

9. Read Ezekiel 34:17-31. Who did God say was to be the new shepherd of Israel after the scattered "sheep" were regathered and had undergone His examination and separation?

10. What would the Lord do for them then?

**THIRD DAY: Read Ezekiel 35 and 36**

11. Read Ezekiel 35. Mount Seir or Edom had been prophesied against several times already in our study of the prophets of Israel. What recent action on their part caused God to have Ezekiel re-emphasize their coming destruction? (See also Ezekiel 36:5.)

12. Read Ezekiel 36:1-15. Though Israel and Judah are now both fallen and their inhabitants taken captive far from their own land, God had Ezekiel prophesy concerning His future plans for their now ravaged homeland. List some of the things God would do in the land of Israel in the future.

13. Read Ezekiel 36:16-30. Not only did God plan to reclaim and renovate the land for His people, but He also planned to change His people so that they could appreciate being returned to the land. List some of the things He promised to do in them and for them. (See also Ezekiel 11:19 and 18:31.)
    (a) in them

    (b) for them

Page 35

# LESSON 14
**PROPHETS OF ISRAEL**

14. Read Ezekiel 36:31-38. The goodness of God in restoring the land and bringing spiritual changes to His people would bring a new awareness to His people and the surrounding nations. Of what would these be aware?
    (a) His people

    (b) the nations

**FOURTH DAY: Read Ezekiel 37**

15. Read Ezekiel 37:1-14. Ezekiel was transported to another place, by the power of the Holy Spirit, to look at a valley full of dry, human bones. Matching:
    _____(a) What did God ask Ezekiel about the bones?
    _____(b) What did Ezekiel wisely answer?
    _____(c) What group did the rejuvenated bones represent?
    _____(d) What did the dry bones symbolize for them?
    _____(e) From where did God call the bones?
    _____(f) What did God promise them?

    1. from their graves which He had opened
    2. the whole house of Israel
    3. *"O Lord GOD, You know."*
    4. *"Our bones are dry, our hope is lost, and we ourselves are cut off!"*
    5. *"Son of man, can these bones live?"*
    6. *"I will put My spirit in you, and you shall live, and I will place you in your own land. Then you shall know that I, the LORD, have spoken it and performed it."*

16. Read Ezekiel 37:15-28. In this new "living parable," what were the two labeled sticks held in one hand supposed to symbolize?

17. When asked about the sticks, what did God have Ezekiel reveal about these aspects of Israel's future?
    (a) their situation in exile

    (b) their form of government

    (c) their new king

    (d) their ownership of the Promised Land

    (e) their place of worship

Page 36

# LESSON 14
## PROPHETS OF ISRAEL

**FIFTH DAY: Read Ezekiel 38 and 39**

18. Read Ezekiel 38:1-13. Ezekiel was told to set his face against a man who would lead a coalition of nations against Israel in the *"latter years."* List all the nations who would participate with him. (**Note:** *"The prince of Rosh"* means "chief prince" and could possibly be part of his title and not a country.)

19. What would make Gog and his confederacy pick that particular time to come against Israel?

20. Read Ezekiel 38:14-23.
    (a) How will God defend His people at that time?

    (b) for what purpose?

21. Read Ezekiel 39:1-8. What additional details were given here about God's defeat of Gog and his troops?

22. Read Ezekiel 39:9-20. Matching:
    _____(a) This is what Israel will use for fuel for seven years instead of cutting wood.
    _____(b) This is where Gog and his defeated troops will be buried.
    _____(c) All the people of Israel will have to work this long to bury all the bodies of their enemies.
    _____(d) A special group will continue to look for unburied remains and will be helped in finding them because of these.
    _____(e) God gave a message through Ezekiel to this group to assemble for a "feast," to help with the disposal of the dead bodies of men and animals.

    1. markers set up by citizens where they found unburied human remains
    2. in a valley in Israel, east of the sea
    3. the weapons of Gog's troops: shields, bucklers, bows, arrows, javelins, spears
    4. seven months
    5. every sort of bird of the air and beast of the field

Page 37

23. Read Ezekiel 39:21-29. Finally, in these latter days, people will understand why God dealt with His people as He did.
    (a) What will the Gentiles realize?

    (b) What will His own people understand?

24. Which of the qualities or actions of God described in these chapters did you find most comforting or surprising? Why?

# Notes

## EZEKIEL 33-39

### Ezekiel Recommissioned (Ezekiel 33:1-11)

In the early chapters of Ezekiel, after the opening vision of God's throne-room, the command to eat the two-sided scroll, and the Holy Spirit's transport of Ezekiel to sit with his fellow captives, God announced something else to Ezekiel: *"Son of man, I have made you a watchman for the house of Israel; therefore hear a word from My mouth, and give them warning from Me"* (Ezekiel 3:17). Very similarly, in the current study of Chapter 33, God repeated this call to Ezekiel, complete with the warning of judgment if he failed to do his job.

Why a second call or recommissioning? Perhaps since Jerusalem had actually fallen (the announcement reached him six months after the fact in verse 21, but God's Spirit had already told him), Ezekiel might have thought his work was finished, but it was not. God had further corrections for Ezekiel to relate to the exiles whom God had, in His mercy, allowed to escape ahead of the disaster in Judah. These people would be the parents of the Jews who would be allowed to return to Judah in seventy years, and they needed to act like it (Jeremiah 29:10). God wanted them to repent of their current sins, that He might spare them from further judgment: *"Say to them: 'As I live,' says the Lord GOD, "I have no pleasure in the death of the wicked, but that the wicked turn from his way and live. Turn, turn, from your evil ways! For why should you die, O house of Israel?'"* (Ezekiel 33:11).

### God Charged with Unfairness (Ezekiel 33:12-20)

Another task for Ezekiel was to correct some wrong-thinking among the exiles. They had been charging God with unfairness in His judgments. Apart from the idea that such accusations were pretty brazen when one considered that they were being made in regard to the Creator of the universe, there was no reason to doubt God's good character or charge Him with inconsistency. God is very consistent: He always forgives the person who repents. It does not matter to Him if a person has been a sinner of the worst kind for decades; if he repents, God will forgive him. Also completely consistent with this is the fact that He will not forgive the unrepentant, even if that person has acted righteously for years beforehand: *"I will judge every one of you according to his own ways."* God's mercy and grace are given with consideration for the current condition of a person's heart. Jesus described similar complaints by the "seemingly" righteous against those coming late to the kingdom in the parable of the prodigal son and older brother in Luke 15:11-32 as well as in the parable about the workers hired at different hours for the same wages in Matthew 20:1-16. God's mercy often seems too good to believe, especially to the ones who believe themselves to be in no real need of it.

### Fall of Jerusalem and Death of Survivors (Ezekiel 33:21-29)

On January 8, 585 B.C., six months after the fact, a survivor from Jerusalem came to Babylon to tell the Jewish exiles about the fall of the city to the forces of Babylon. In fulfillment of God's earlier word, this all transpired, even the removal of the periodic **muteness** that had been put on Ezekiel earlier, as a sign to the exiles. (See Ezekiel 3:26,27; 24:26,27.)

Not all the inhabitants of Jerusalem had been killed or captured when the city fell, but the Holy Spirit revealed to Ezekiel that the survivors had misinterpreted their initial deliverance. They were boasting that they, certainly superior to their forefather Abraham who *"was only one,"* would set about repossessing their covenant land. Shockingly, after all their trials and tribulations, they still remained unhumbled and unrepentant, blind to their own wickedness and unaware that their actions had helped **precipitate** the horrible judgment by the Babylonians.

Ezekiel was told to speak against their sins of paganism, idolatry, murder, and adultery. God did not intend for such wicked people to now inherit the promises He had made to Abraham; He intended for them to die for their sins. Those in the rubble of the city would be killed by the sword; those in the surrounding fields would be eaten by wild beasts; and those hiding in strongholds and caves would be cut down by disease and pestilence. God's judgment would be complete: all *"arrogant strength"* would be stopped. Then, finally, men would see that the Lord was in charge of the cleansing of His land; He would successfully remove all those who, without repentance, had committed abominations within its borders.

## Ezekiel the Celebrity (Ezekiel 33:30-33)

God gave a personal word of caution to His servant Ezekiel. Evidently with the confirmed fulfillment of all the prophecies Ezekiel had been giving during the past seven years, he had gained a certain celebrity-status among his fellow exiles. Everyone was talking about him and inviting others to come and hear him. However, God warned Ezekiel that although they were enjoying him, much as one does a lovely new song, they were not really taking him seriously: *"...they hear your words, but they do not do them; for with their mouth they show much love, but their hearts pursue their own gain"* (Ezekiel 33:31). God did not want Ezekiel distracted by his sudden popularity; it would soon pass away.

## Selfish Shepherds (Ezekiel 34:1-10, 17-21)

Now that Jerusalem had fallen and Judah had been taken over by Babylon, God inspired Ezekiel to reveal one of the primary causes—selfish leadership. Directed at the former and possibly current shepherds of Israel, Ezekiel's words were blunt revelations of their failures. They had fed and clothed themselves extravagantly but neglected to care for the flocks under their charge. The basic needs were not even supplied, while cruelty was employed to rule them. (The word for cruelty here was the same as used in Exodus 1:11 where the Egyptian taskmasters afflicted the Israelites.) Without protection or direction, the residents of Israel had been scattered and left vulnerable to outside attack. God saw all this and hated it; He would permanently remove such selfish shepherds from their positions. He would act as Judge over them, punishing those who not only greedily took the best for themselves but also polluted what they did not use so that others could not enjoy what was left (Ezekiel 34:17-21). The last four kings of Judah certainly experienced God's judgment as He allowed the Egyptians and Babylonians to take them down from their places of leadership (2 Chronicles 36).

## God, the Good Shepherd (Ezekiel 34:11-16, 22-31)

After promising the removal of the selfish shepherds, God vowed to fill the void in leadership Himself. At a future time, God would seek out His sheep from all the countries to which they had been scattered and bring them back to His good fold on the mountains of Israel. He personally would strengthen the weak and heal the sick. In that day they would no longer be vulnerable to enemy attacks (Ezekiel 34:22) but would be led by God's chosen shepherd David (Ezekiel 34:24).

Most Bible scholars think this was a reference to Messiah (Jesus), the seed of David, who would return from heaven to rule over Israel in the end-times. This view is supported with the references to God's promise of an eternal throne, not to David himself, but to the offspring of David, whom numerous Scriptures declare to be Jesus (1 Chronicles 17:7-14; John 7:42). However, some think, because David is named without qualification several times (Ezekiel 34:23,24; 37:24,25), that his appointment should be taken literally. This view holds that a resurrected David would return to rule, in the same way Moses was allowed to appear to speak with Jesus on the Mount of Transfiguration centuries after his death. (See Matthew 17:3.) One day we will know for sure!

Revelation 20 described a thousand-year reign of Christ on earth, commonly referred to as the Millennium. Ezekiel's prophecies seem to speak of the same era, particularly God's promises about the regathering of the scattered flock of Israel, the removal of wild animals (Ezekiel 34:25), and the causing of **unprecedented** productivity in the farming operations in that area. (See Isaiah 11:1-10.) With all these blessings, those living then will know for certain that God is their God and realize that He is the only truly Good Shepherd.

## Another Prophecy Against Edom (Ezekiel 35)

Mount Seir was synonymous with Edom, and here Ezekiel prophesied again about coming judgment on that nation. Actually related to Israel (Esau, also known as Edom, was the twin brother of Jacob, also known as Israel), Edom kept alive an *"ancient hatred"* for Israel and actually *"shed the blood of the children of Israel...at the time of their calamity"* with Babylon (Ezekiel 35:5). They also boasted that they would confiscate the lands of Israel and Judah now that the inhabitants of both nations had been exiled to distant lands. God took their actions against His people very personally and swore to leave them as desolate as they had hoped Israel would be.

Edom was one of the most prophesied-against nations in the Bible. Because of their kinship to Israel and their shared heritage with Abraham, they should have known better than to oppose the covenant out-workings of Jehovah. They should have known they could not bully their way back into ownership of their lost birthright. Repentance could have opened the door for them into the covenant but not brute force. The countries surrounding modern Israel today should take heed to the history of Edom. Opposition to God's covenant people has never paid. (For other prophecies against Edom see Isaiah 34:5, Jeremiah 49:17; Ezekiel 25:12,13; Joel 3:19; Amos 1:11, Obadiah 1:1; and Malachi 1:4.)

## The Land Revitalized, the People Renewed (Ezekiel 36)

Since the prophecies had been fulfilled that related to the fall of Jerusalem, the selfish shepherds chastised and the ancient foes of Edom condemned, Ezekiel was now free to receive and reveal God's plans for the future of Israel, that tract of land that featured so prominently in God's promises to Abraham. Though at that time desolate because of years of war and seemingly forsaken to the eyes of the surrounding nations, Israel was still God's special land, the place He had chosen to put His name. He would soon show those who wanted to take it for themselves that He was still in charge of it.

God told Ezekiel to speak to the mountains of Israel, promising them a future lushness and a return of their rightful inhabitants. Since God had promised the land to Abraham and his descendants forever, the absence of those descendants from the land was a negative reflection on God Himself. Even though He had to remove His people from the land because *"they defiled it by their own ways and deeds,"*—deeds so despicable God compared them to the discharge of a menstruating woman—God would one day return a righteous remnant to that land to clear His own good Name and make good on His eternal promises to Abraham (Ezekiel 36:17-24).

So as to make certain that history did not repeat itself, God made clear that the regathered children of Israel who would be allowed to come back to the land to enjoy the restored lushness and guaranteed peace would have to be righteous covenant-keepers. To make sure of that, God would personally cleanse them from their sins, give them new hearts and new spirits, and give them each His own Holy Spirit to cause them once and for all to walk in His statutes and keep His commandments (Ezekiel 36:25-27).

The result of this spiritual renewal would be that His people would finally be able to enjoy the full benefits of their relationship to Him and the Garden-of-Eden loveliness He would restore to their land. To these people, God further promised to *"increase their men like a flock."* It would appear that a "baby-boom" would be another indication of God's pleasure with His renewed people.

When would all this occur? Most conservative scholars believe that these things will occur during the Millennium, described in Revelation 20. Even though there has been a modern-day return of Jews to their homeland in Israel, the condition of the land—though better than it has been for years—and the spiritual awareness of the people do not at all match Ezekiel's description in this chapter of the future of the nation. So we wait and watch for God to fulfill the things He has promised for that land and that people. He will do it exactly as He has said.

## Dry Bones Live (Ezekiel 37:1-15)

Probably one of the most well-known chapters in Ezekiel, Chapter 37 described a startling experience the prophet had when he was again transported *"in the Spirit"* to take part in another educational field trip. Ezekiel was set down in the middle of a large, unnamed valley in which there were *"very many"* bones which were *"very dry."* The indication was that they had been there for a long, long time. Also, the fact that the bones had not been buried seemed to point to a shameful defeat by their enemies, persons so full of hate that they denied their victims even the most perfunctory of burials.

Ezekiel was told that the bones represented the *"whole house of Israel"* (Ezekiel 37:11). God asked him if they could live. Ezekiel, well aware of the power of God, humbly replied, *"O Lord GOD, You know"* (Ezekiel 37:3). God told Ezekiel to prophesy to the bones because He intended to bring them back to life. And so He did: muscles, flesh, and skin—all but breath. Some see this as an indication of a two-phase program of Israel's regathering. First, a physical regathering in the land followed later by a separate, spiritual renewal. Anyway, in the account, Ezekiel was employed to call for the four winds to fill the men; the wind (the same word in Hebrew for spirit) came, and the men stood and lived, forming a very great army. God had a future plan—to resurrect a dead nation and bring its citizens back into their own land, calling them right out of the "graves" of foreign exile.

## Two Made One (Ezekiel 37:16-28)

In this section Ezekiel revealed God's plan to reunite Israel and Judah into one nation, as they had been at first. With the aid of two labeled sticks held in one hand, Ezekiel was to teach the people about God's future plans for them. **Reiterating** what had been revealed before, Ezekiel declared that the future reunited nation would have one king; He would be God's servant David. In that day they would enjoy a covenant of peace with God and would have God's sanctuary rebuilt among them. The restoration of God's sanctuary would be the final proof to the surrounding nations that God had sanctified Israel once and for all.

## Gog Leads an Attack on Israel (Ezekiel 38 and 39)

These are also well-known chapters for prophecy lovers. In them was described a battle to be fought *"in the latter years"* (Ezekiel 38:8) when the forces led by a leader named Gog will muster for attack against God's regathered people living in peace in Israel. Apparently, Israel's relaxed security (*"unwalled villages"* and cities *"having neither bars nor gates"*) will make her appear to be an easy target for her enemies. Gog will lead his amassed troops out of the far north, all riding on horses, to come against Israel. God revealed that He will have actually instigated the confrontation so that He might have His power revealed to the world.

The battle will be decidedly one-sided. At the onset, God will order such a great earthquake in the land of Israel that every living thing on earth will be shaken: *"The mountains shall be thrown down, the steep places shall fall, and every wall shall fall to the ground."* Then God will cause confusion among Gog's forces so that they turn their swords on each other. As if that were not enough, God will send pestilence, flooding rain, huge hailstones, along with fire and brimstone from heaven. Gog's army will be completely destroyed and the world will know that the supernatural power of God brought it about.

In Chapter 39, Ezekiel continued the description of Gog's defeat. Gog and his troops will die on the mountains of Israel, and God will invite the birds of prey and **carnivorous** beasts of the area to gather to devour the bodies. In the meantime, God will send fire on Gog's headquarters at Magog and on his supporters who live on the coastlands. They, too, will recognize God's power.

The **armaments** left by Gog's forces will be so numerous that it will take Israel seven years to use them up as fuel. The bones of the corpses that had been picked clean by the scavenging creatures will be buried in a valley *"east of the sea"* (whether this is the Mediterranean or the Dead Sea is not indicated), making such a huge pile that the roadways will be obstructed, stopping normal travel. It will take seven months for the appointed officials

# LESSON 14 — PROPHETS OF ISRAEL

to finish the disposal of bones, but a follow-up group will still have to scour the country for missing parts that, left unburied, would defile the land.

## Who and When?

That was a synopsis of events, but most prophecy-lovers want to know more. Who is Gog and who are his allies? When will this confrontation occur? These are not questions that can be answered with certainty; many very reliable Bible expositors disagree on the answers, but here are some insights.

First, the name Magog was listed as one of the grandsons of Noah in Genesis 10:2, but that fact does not help establish the identity of a place called Magog in Ezekiel. Some think Magog may simply mean "place of Gog" and indicate an unknown location far to the north of Israel. In Revelation 20:7-10, John described the last battle of the world in which Satan, loosed from his thousand-year imprisonment, is freed to rally Gog and Magog (described as *"the nations which are in the four corners of the earth"*) to go up and surround the saints at Jerusalem to attack them. However, as in Ezekiel's account of Gog's confrontation with Israel, God will intervene to stop it before it starts. However, in John's account, God will stop it instantaneously with fire from heaven sent to devour all Satan's forces.

The use of Gog and Magog by Ezekiel and John are certainly not coincidental. While the two prophets seem to be describing similar but not identical events, we are to see some connections. Both battles serve to show the absolute power of God over the enemies of His people and that He can completely fulfill all His promises to Israel despite what man or Satan orchestrate to stop Him.

The identity of Gog cannot be established clearly. Some of the nations listed as his allies in Ezekiel 38 can be recognized, while others cannot. First, "Rosh" should probably be translated "chief prince" and be seen as part of Gog's title. Meshech and Tubal have been identified with various places. In recent commentaries, because of new linguistic studies, Meshech is identified with the Assyrian "Mushku," south of Gomer in central Asia Minor (Ezekiel 27:13) and Tubal with the Assyrian "Tabab," a city south of Togarmah in eastern Asia Minor. A different view, however, was made popular in the *Scofield Reference Bible,* published years ago. There Rosh is identified as Russia with Meshech and Tubal as corresponding with Moscow and Tobolsk. Iain M. Duguid, author of *The NIV Application Commentary on Ezekiel* summarized the problem of differing identifications in this way:

> However, even if correct identifications were to be made on the basis of sound linguistic and archaeological data, attempts to isolate *particular* nations as "Israel's last enemies" fly in the face of what the text is saying. The point of Ezekiel 38-39 is not that at some distant point in future history these particular nations will oppose Israel, while others (America? Britain?) will rally to her aid. Rather, these seven nations from the ends of the earth, from all four points of the compass, represent symbolically a supreme attempt by the united forces of evil to crush the peace of God's people. This, not coincidentally, is the same interpretation given to "Gog and Magog" in Revelation 20:8. They represent "the nations of the four corners of the earth" whom Satan gathers for the final battle against God's people, the city he loves. Their defeat in Revelation is the prerequisite for the establishment of the new Jerusalem, the heavenly city of Revelation 21, which itself has many points of contact with Ezekiel's visionary temple in Ezekiel 40-48 (Duguid, p. 453,454).

Some of Gog's other allies in Ezekiel's prophecies are still identifiable. Persia held the land now known as Iran, Cush became modern Ethiopia (south of Egypt), and Put became Libya in North Africa. So although God calls the enemies down from the far north (Ezekiel 38:6), the nations listed represent enemies north, south, east, and west of Israel.

They are said to be attracted to the battle against Israel because she will be living in a time of relaxed security. Any student of Israel's history knows that there has not yet been a time when she has enjoyed relaxed security. Most of her gross national product to this day goes for defense. However, there are two times in the Scriptures when such a time of security is prophesied. The first, as will be discussed in Daniel, will be when the Antichrist signs a seven-year peace covenant with Israel. The next will be during the Millennium when Christ rules over Israel Himself. Ezekiel's prophecy of a war with Gog seems to fit into the first time of peace and is thought by some to be God's supernatural defense of her that will shock a depraved world just prior to the Tribulation. John's prophecy of a battle with Gog is thought to fit in best with the second time of promised relaxed security, after the thousand-year reign of Christ when Satan is loosed one last time.

## Short Summation for a Long Lesson

Whoever the enemy, they will never successfully undermine God's will. He has made promises to Israel that He will keep. He chastised His covenant people for their many sins, but He has decreed that they will be brought back: *"And I will not hide My face from them any more; for I shall have poured out My Spirit on the house of Israel."* Woe to the people who try to curse the ones He has commanded to be blessed. The timing of the fulfillment of His prophecies is completely in His hands. He has told us His plans so that we do not have to fear the future, because through Christ we can always be found on His side—the winning side—forever.

## VOCABULARY

1. **armaments:** military supplies and weapons
2. **carnivorous:** flesh-eating
3. **muteness:** condition of being unable to speak
4. **precipitate:** cause something to happen by an earlier action or comment
5. **reiterating:** saying or doing something over and over again
6. **unprecedented:** unique, not following a previous rule or example

# Notes

# Notes

# PROPHETS OF ISRAEL — LESSON 15

## Daily Bible Study Questions

**Study Procedure:** Read the Scripture references before answering questions. Unless otherwise instructed, use the Bible only in answering questions. Some questions may be more difficult than others but try to answer as many as you can. Pray for God's wisdom and understanding as you study and don't be discouraged if some answers are not obvious at first.

**THIS WEEK'S MEMORY VERSE:**

(Ezekiel 48:35) *"...and the name of the city from that day shall be: THE LORD IS THERE."*

**FIRST DAY: Review of Ezekiel 33-39**

1. Multiple choice:

    (a) Ezekiel was recommissioned to be God's
       1. prophet.   2. watchman.   3. judge over the people of Israel.

    (b) These were accused of causing the fall of Israel.
       1. the Egyptians   2. the false prophets   3. the selfish shepherds

    (c) One of the most condemned nations, this was synonymous with Mount Seir.
       1. Edom   2. Isaac   3. Moab

    (d) God promised these things to a regathered Israel at a future time.
       1. lush growth in all agriculture   2. a place of honor among nations
       3. a new heart and a new spirit   4. an increase in population

    (e) What did the dry bones represent?
       1. the defeated armies of Gog   2. the whole house of Israel   3. judgment on Edom

    (f) Which of these was not included in the list of Gog's allies?
       1. Libya (Put)   2. Ethiopia (Cush)   3. Meshech   4. Assyria   5. Gomer
       6. Togarmah   7. Persia   8. Tubal

2. What did you find puzzling, interesting, or convicting from last week's lesson?

**SECOND DAY: Read Ezekiel 40:1-43:5**

3. Read Ezekiel 40:1-6. Just as the book of Ezekiel opened with a vision, its last section, written twenty years later, closed with one. Summarize what Ezekiel saw here.

# LESSON 15

**PROPHETS OF ISRAEL**

4. Some of the dimensions of the things Ezekiel described about the temple and some of the boundaries later given for the re-allotment of the land to the individual twelve tribes would not fit on the present topography of Israel. What did we have in last week's lesson that will have significantly altered Israel's landscape to accommodate the plans and dimensions of structures in this new vision?

5. Scan the specifications recorded of this future temple in the rest of Chapter 40 and in 41 and 42. Refer to the picture below. If you have studied the tabernacle or temple before, what did you notice that was missing from this one or was different about this one?

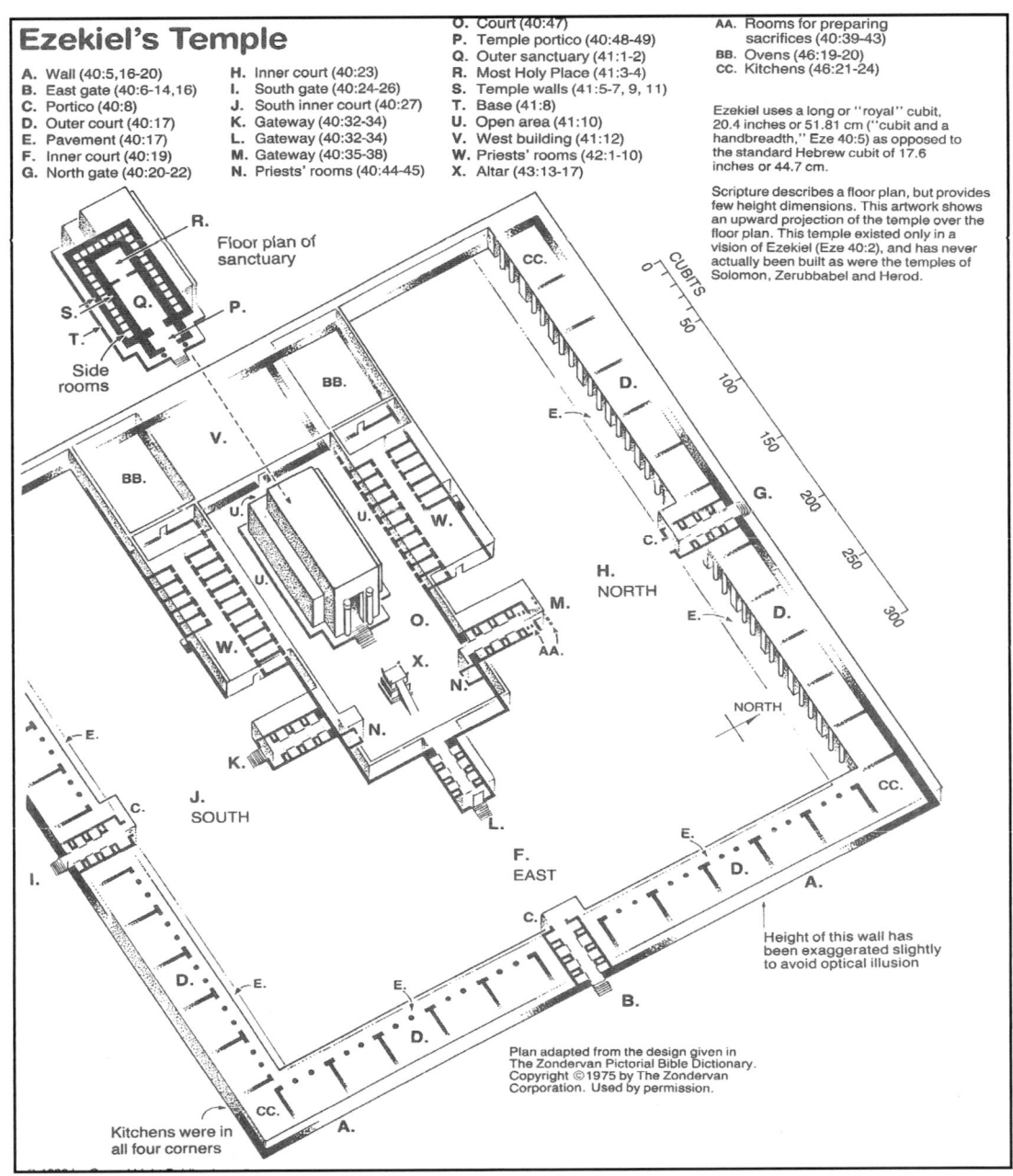

Permission Pending © 1989 Gospel Light Publications.

# LESSON 15  PROPHETS OF ISRAEL

6. Read Ezekiel 43:1-5. Review Ezekiel 10:18 and 11:23. What happy event did Ezekiel get to foresee?

**THIRD DAY: Read Ezekiel 43:6-44:3**

7. Read Ezekiel 43:6-12.
   (a) What did God say about the temple?

   (b) How long would this temple last?

   (c) What did God intend for the description of this temple to cause in the people who heard about it from Ezekiel?

8. Read Ezekiel 43:13-27.
   (a) This passage describes the altar and the proper ceremonies for its dedication. Considering this, what were to be the main activities in this future temple?

   (b) What do you think about this if this temple was to be for the far future?

9. Read Ezekiel 44:1-3. Why would the east gate be kept shut?

10. Ezekiel mentions *"the prince."* Some who study Scripture think this prince is Jesus. Read the following verses and defend or oppose that position with what you find.
    (a) (Ezekiel 44:2,3) *"And the LORD said to me, 'This gate shall be shut; it shall not be opened, and no man shall enter by it, because the LORD God of Israel has entered by it; therefore it shall be shut. As for the prince, because he is the prince, he may sit in it to eat bread before the LORD; he shall enter by way of the vestibule of the gateway, and go out the same way.'"*

Page 49

# LESSON 15

**PROPHETS OF ISRAEL**

(b) (Ezekiel 45:22) *"And on that day the prince shall prepare for himself and for all the people of the land a bull for a sin offering."*

(c) (Ezekiel 46:2) *"The prince shall enter by way of the vestibule of the gateway from the outside, and stand by the gatepost. The priests shall prepare his burnt offering and his peace offerings. He shall worship at the threshold of the gate. Then he shall go out, but the gate shall not be shut until evening."*

(d) (Ezekiel 46:16-18) *"Thus says the Lord GOD: 'If the prince gives a gift of some of his inheritance to any of his sons, it shall belong to his sons; it is their possession by inheritance. But if he gives a gift of some of his inheritance to one of his servants, it shall be his until the year of liberty, after which it shall return to the prince. But his inheritance shall belong to his sons; it shall become theirs. Moreover the prince shall not take any of the people's inheritance by evicting them from their property; he shall provide an inheritance for his sons from his own property, so that none of My people may be scattered from his property.'"*

## FOURTH DAY: Read Ezekiel 44:4-47:12

11. Read Ezekiel 44:4-31. What was to be the purpose for all the strict regulations on the sons of Zadok who served as priests?

12. Read Chapters 45 and 46. What feasts or sacred days will still be observed in the future temple?

13. Why do you think God had Ezekiel record all these detailed ordinances for correct worship? (Consider the time in which Ezekiel was living in your answer.)

# LESSON 15 — PROPHETS OF ISRAEL

14. Read Ezekiel 47:1-12. What new thing was Ezekiel shown in this vision, and what effects did it have on the area? (See also Joel 3:18; Zechariah 13:1 and 14:8.)

## FIFTH DAY: Read Ezekiel 47:13-48:35

15. Read Ezekiel 47:13-23. In these new borders of Israel, how were strangers assigned a place to live?

16. What section of land was no longer included? (**Hint:** It was where 2 1/2 tribes had stopped short of their inheritance. See Numbers 32.)

17. Read Ezekiel 48. What did you find interesting about the division of the land among the twelve tribes?

18. In the list of the twelve tribes for whom the gates of the city were named, what happened to Ephraim and Manasseh?

19. Consider the name of the city, *"The Lord Is There."* How does it make a fitting conclusion to these last end-time prophecies of Ezekiel?

20. What has most impressed or challenged you from the whole study of the prophecies of Ezekiel?

# Ezekiel 40-48

## Transported in the Spirit Again (Ezekiel 40:1-5)

Chapters 40 through 48 form the last section of Ezekiel's prophecies and contain his final recorded vision. It had been twenty-five years since his group of exiles had come to Babylon from Judah, and the *"hand of the Lord"* came upon him on the tenth day of the first month of that twenty-fifth year. If Ezekiel were using the **ecclesiastical** calendar here, then this was the annual date, back when the temple still stood, that they would have selected the lamb for Passover in preparation for that week-long commemoration of the exodus. As a priest, perhaps Ezekiel had been thinking or praying about their situation on that day, so far removed from their old way of life. Anyway, in a vision, the Lord transported Ezekiel to Israel, placed him on a very high mountain, and showed him what looked *"like the structure of a city."* For an exiled people, with years yet to go before they could return home, this scene of a rebuilt Jerusalem would have been comforting. For a priest like Ezekiel, the vision of a rebuilt and enlarged temple would have been inspiring, providing strong motivation to persevere.

With a bronze-skinned man carrying measuring instruments, most likely an angel, Ezekiel set out for a closer look at the place he had seen from a distance. He was told to see, hear, and focus intently on all the details, so that he might be able to *"declare to the house of Israel everything"* he saw (Ezekiel 40:4). The line of flax, or fibrous string, carried by Ezekiel's guide would be used to measure long spans; the measuring rod, roughly ten feet long, was for shorter spans. A cubit, mentioned in some of the subsequent dimensions, was the distance from elbow to fingertip, about eighteen inches; a cubit and a handbreadth (Ezekiel 40:5) was about twenty-one inches. An artist's rendering given in the questions' section should help make clear the detailed description Ezekiel recorded in these chapters. The foot/mile equivalents will be given in these notes from time to time to help in visualization.

## The Temple Structure Described (Ezekiel 40:6-42:20 and 43:13-27)

1. **The Eastern Gate** (Ezekiel 40:6-16): There were three gates for entering the temple area in the center of the city, but the first to be described was the eastern gate, through which the Lord Himself would enter to fill the place with His glory. After that event, the gate would be closed in respect for that holy moment. The area surrounding the temple itself was elevated, and the gateways were approached by steps leading to two successive thresholds, each ten by ten feet. Rather elaborate entryways they were, with gate chambers joined by archways leading to a vestibule, all accented with beveled windows. On the outside, each gatepost was adorned with a palm tree, a common decorative motif of the East (1 Kings 6:29).

2. **The Outer Court of the Temple** (Ezekiel 40:17-19): Having entered the eastern gate, Ezekiel observed the outer court of the temple. Thirty chambers lined the perimeter, but they were placed only on the north, east, and south sides of the complex.

3. **The Northern Gate and Southern Gate** (Ezekiel 40:20-27): These were identical to the eastern gate in design but in their description was added one more bit of information: there were seven steps leading up to each gate.

4. **The Gateways to the Inner Court** (Ezekiel 40:28-37): Directly across from each outer-court gate was a corresponding and identically designed inner-court gateway which led into the area nearest the temple itself.

5. **The Places for Preparation of Sacrifices** (Ezekiel 40:38-43): Chambers to prepare sacrifices were placed inside these gateways. Tables of stone for slaughtering and preparing sacrifices were arranged in this area. Instruments for cutting and hooks for hanging the carcasses were put there also.

6. **Chambers for Singers and Priests** (Ezekiel 40:44-46): Changing rooms for priests and singers were provided outside the inner gates.

7. **The Sanctuary or Temple** (Chapter 41): The temple itself was elevated about ten feet higher than the rest of the complex. It was entered on the east by steps leading up to a wide entryway. The pattern and dimensions of the actual temple were very similar to Solomon's. The dimensions of the whole sanctuary were 70x35 feet, with the holy of holies being a square of 35x35 feet. There were side chambers built on the outer walls of the temple itself that ascended like stairsteps to make three stories. A building for the priests' use was attached to the western side of the temple. The galleries around the temple area were paneled with wood and decorated with carvings of two-faced cherubim and palm trees. A wooden altar was described (Ezekiel 41:22) as being in the temple and was designated as the one placed *"before the LORD."* This was thought to correspond to the table of showbread sometimes called the table of Presence, which represented the tribes of Israel in its presentation of the twelve loaves of bread (Exodus 25:23-30). Interestingly, no mention was made of the ark of the covenant, the mercy seat, the altar of incense, or the golden lampstand.

8. **The Chambers for the Priests** (Ezekiel 42:1-14): Special additional chambers in which the priests would eat the designated offerings were described here. They would also serve as changing rooms for the priests to get in and out of their priestly garments.

9. **Courtyard Dimensions** (Ezekiel 42:15-20): Each of the walls of the outer court of the temple were 875 feet long. These were to separate the holy precincts of the temple area from the city beyond.

10. **The Altar** (Ezekiel 43:13-27): A description was given for a large, elevated altar on which the sacrifices would be properly burned. The details for its consecration were given, essential for its purification and use.

## The Glory Returns (Ezekiel 43:1-9)

Here Ezekiel recorded what must have been the most wonderful experience of his life—the return of the glory of the Lord to fill His temple. Ezekiel had witnessed the departing of God's glory in the early years of his ministry (Ezekiel 11:23), and now he saw it return the same way it had left, through the eastern gate. This vision was God's promise that He not only would forgive His people but also replace them in their land and provide them with one last temple in which they could resume their proper worship.

Just as he had seen before, Ezekiel saw the presence of God and heard Him speak: *"Son of man, this is the place of My throne and the place of the soles of My feet, where I will dwell in the midst of the children of Israel forever. No more shall the house of Israel defile My holy name, they nor their kings, by their harlotry or with the carcasses of their kings on the their high places"* (Ezekiel 43:7).

## Purpose of This Temple (Ezekiel 43:10-12)

God instructed Ezekiel to reveal this vision about the temple to the people of Israel that they might be ashamed of their past sinfulness. How this would come about was not explained; however, at a time when the Jews had been away from the temple in Jerusalem for twenty-five years and had known of its destruction for fourteen years, this reminder of the pattern and purpose of the temple might easily awaken in them a desire to return to a right relationship with their God. To those indicating real repentance, Ezekiel was to relate all these details so they might *"keep its whole design and all its ordinances, and perform them"* (Ezekiel 43:11). This was the first revealed purpose of this vision.

While the outer and inner courts had three gateways, the temple itself had only one entrance, which was by way of the altar of sacrifice, on which acceptable offerings had to be made. There were stages of approach. First, proper blood sacrifice was needed, mediated by an approved priest, and offered to the Lord on behalf of the repentant offerer. Then, following specific laws, the priests came nearer to the presence of the Lord through the holy place itself. Mention was made in Ezekiel's vision of neither an active high priest nor placement of the ark, the mercy seat, or even the dividing curtain outside the holy of holies. In contrast, in the original Scriptural directions, the high priest annually pulled back the veil, sprinkled the mercy seat on the ark with blood in atonement for his and the people's sins, and entered into the very holy of holies. The absence of these articles, to some, indicate that the sacrifices here were meant to be memorial in nature, reminding the worshipers of what would in the future already have been accomplished by their true High Priest, Messiah. Thus the presence of another high priest or the mercy seat was not necessary.

## Placement in Time of This Temple

This brings up the varying views about the placement of this temple in a time context. First, some think that the vision of this temple was not a prophecy of an actual future temple but a motivational tool to inspire the captives in exile to hold on to their faith. That view would be supported by Ezekiel 43:10,11 alluded to above. Next, some, who accept that as partially the reason for the vision, go further to assert that Ezekiel was given this plan, much as Moses had been given the original plan for the tabernacle on Mount Sinai, so that it actually could be built when the exiles were allowed to return to Jerusalem at the conclusion of their seventy-year sentence. The problem with this view is that the temple which the returning exiles did build did not follow this pattern at all; it was just a less **ornate** version of Solomon's (Ezra 3:12,13). Another view is that this temple would be built in the end-times so as to exist during the Great Tribulation, since a temple is prophesied as existing at that time (2 Thessalonians 2:3,4). The problem with that view is that God promised Ezekiel that He would keep His presence in this temple forever (Ezekiel 43:7), while the temple which is to exist in the seven last years will be desecrated by the Antichrist who will make all proper sacrifices cease. The last of the more common views is that this temple will be built for use during the thousand-year reign of Christ described in Revelation 20 as a place of worship for the children of Israel living at that time. This view would make sense of the omission of high priest, dividing curtain, and mercy seat. They would not be needed because Christ will already have become their eternal High Priest, who will have opened up the way of mercy for all who come in His name and trust in His sacrifice. The other parts of the vision of Ezekiel in this section, especially the new division of the land among the twelve tribes of Israel in east-to-west allotments, seem better to fit into the boundaries and topography of the Millennial period as well.

The chronological placement of Ezekiel's temple is not essential to anyone's salvation, so be kind when discussing it. At least one of God's purposes for it was made clear: to cause His people to repent from their wickedness through the review of His merciful provision for their sins. Does a review of Christ's great actions on our behalf still have the power to move us to repentance? Does the contemplation of His suffering or the glorious hope of His resurrection move us? Let's hope so.

## The Prince (Ezekiel 44:1-3; 45:6-17; 46:16-24)

A prince was mentioned several times by Ezekiel as the recognized leader of civil government. He was not allowed access to the temple as a priest but was recognized as being worthy of distinctive placement in the eastern gateway as a high official. Some commentators confidently identify him as Jesus, but several descriptive details prohibit this view. First, he is not deemed worthy to enter the temple in the same way the glory came in (Ezekiel 44:2,3). He is not deity; Jesus is. Next, in the division of land, the princes are warned not to oppress the people (Ezekiel 45:8); Jesus would never oppress the people. Further, the prince receives offerings from the people and then is responsible for seeing that the proper offerings are provided for the temple (Ezekiel 45:17). Jesus offered Himself one time and sat down on the right hand of the Father (Hebrews 10:11,12). Also, the prince in Ezekiel's vision is warned about the laws of inheritance in regarding his sons (Ezekiel 46:16-18). Jesus was not married and has no sons. Therefore, it appears that the prince will be a recognized leader of the people of Israel at a future time, and the attention given him here should not be surprising. In every age God insists on organization and proper lines of authority to be followed for those holding positions of leadership.

## Those Allowed to Enter (Ezekiel 44:4-9)

Ezekiel again fell on his face in the presence of the glory of the Lord, but he was soon able to hear the Lord's words concerning those allowed inside this temple he had been touring: *"No foreigner, uncircumcised in heart or uncircumcised in flesh, shall enter My sanctuary, including any foreigner who is among the children of Israel."* Evidently, this was to be a strictly Jewish place of worship, having the further distinction of only allowing the truly spiritual children of Abraham to enter.

## The Sons of Zadok (Ezekiel 44:10-31)

Trouble among the priesthood started long before even the idolatrous practices of Ezekiel's time. The high priest at the time of David was a Levite, from the family of Aaron, named Zadok. When his co-worker Abiathar, from another branch of Aaron's family through Eli, committed treason in supporting Adonijah for the throne instead of Solomon, God's choice, his priestly line was marked for punishment (1 Kings 1:7,8). [Eli's line had earlier been prophesied to die out because of the sins of his sons (1 Samuel 2:27-35).] In Ezekiel's vision, God fulfilled all this. Only the priests from Zadok's line could continue to minister before the Lord. All other priests and Levites were allowed only to perform the preparatory and menial tasks of the temple.

Proper behavior, dress, moral righteousness, and even Scriptural eating habits for the priesthood were emphasized in this passage. The priests were to live distinctively, according to God's directions, and serve as models and teachers for the people as to the difference between clean and unclean living (Ezekiel 44:23).

## Setting Aside a Holy District (Ezekiel 45:1-5)

Refer to the sketch below to get a visual-aid for the dividing up of the land around the temple. God was doing everything decently and in order in this special city.

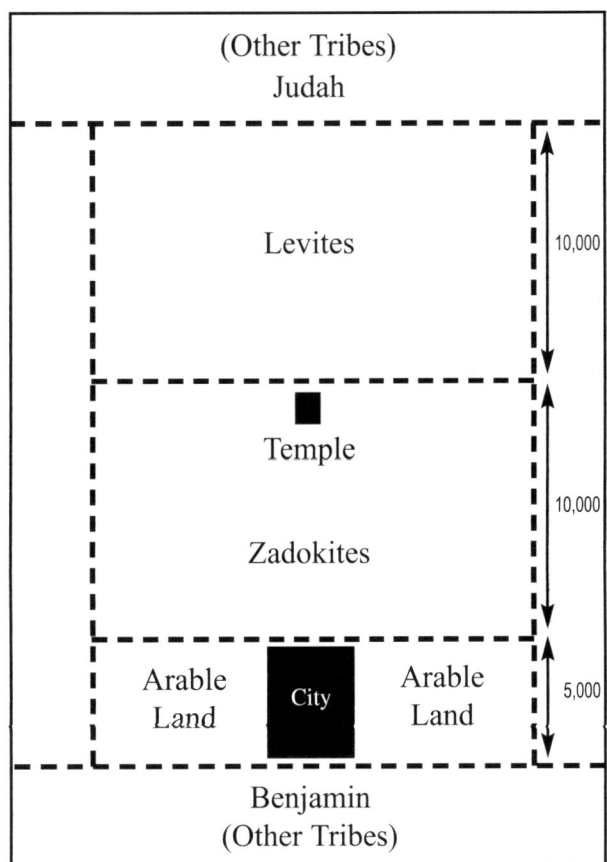

Permission Pending ©1999 Illustration taken from *The NIV Application Commentary: Ezekiel* by Iain M. Duguid (p.516).

## Observing the Old Feasts and Holy Days (Ezekiel 45:18-25; 46:1-15)

Two of the seven feasts for which attendance was mandatory in Leviticus 23 were also required by God to be celebrated in this new temple: Passover and the Feast of Tabernacles. Why those two and not the rest was not made clear.

Sabbaths and New Moons were to be regularly remembered as well, with the details about proper observance given here.

## River of Life (Ezekiel 47:1-12)

As sort of a finishing touch to the hopeful vision of a future place where God will always dwell with His covenant people, Ezekiel was shown a river flowing *"from under the right side of the temple, south of the altar."* At thousand-cubit increments, he was shown its increasing depth.

From its banks grew year-round-producing fruit trees, with healing in their leaves. Wherever the water reached—even into the Dead Sea—the waters became healthy, which was evidenced by the great abundance of fish.

Other prophets had foreseen this same phenomenon:

(Joel 3:18) *"And it will come to pass in that day that the mountains shall drip with new wine, the hills shall flow with milk, and all the brooks of Judah shall be flooded with water; a fountain shall flow from the house of the LORD and water the Valley of Acacias."*

(Zechariah 14:8) *"And in that day it shall be that living waters shall flow from Jerusalem, half of them toward the eastern sea and half of them toward the western sea; in both summer and winter it shall occur."*

(Revelation 22:1-3) *"And he showed me a pure river of water of life, clear as crystal, proceeding from the throne of God and of the Lamb. In the middle of its street, and on either side of the river, was the tree of life, which bore twelve fruits, each tree yielding its fruit every month. The leaves of the tree were for the healing of the nations. And there shall be no more curse, but the throne of God and of the Lamb shall be in it, and His servants shall serve Him."*

## Borders of the Future (Ezekiel 47:13-23)

Quite similar to the borders given in Numbers 34:1,2 but much larger than the boundaries of present-day Israel, the dimensions of this future Israel were given. Much more land northward and southward was to be given than they have today; however, the territory they had inhabited prior to the exile, east of the Jordan, would no longer be included within their borders. While strangers would not be allowed to worship in the new temple (Ezekiel 44:9), they would be allowed to live among the twelve tribes in the newly defined borders of the nation (Ezekiel 47:22,23).

## New Tribal Allotments (Ezekiel 48:1-29)

Consult the map below to see the new configuration of land allotments for the twelve tribes of Israel. In this plan, Ephraim and Manasseh, sons of Joseph, would inherit equally with their uncles, and the Levites and priests would be given a special district of their own in which to reside.

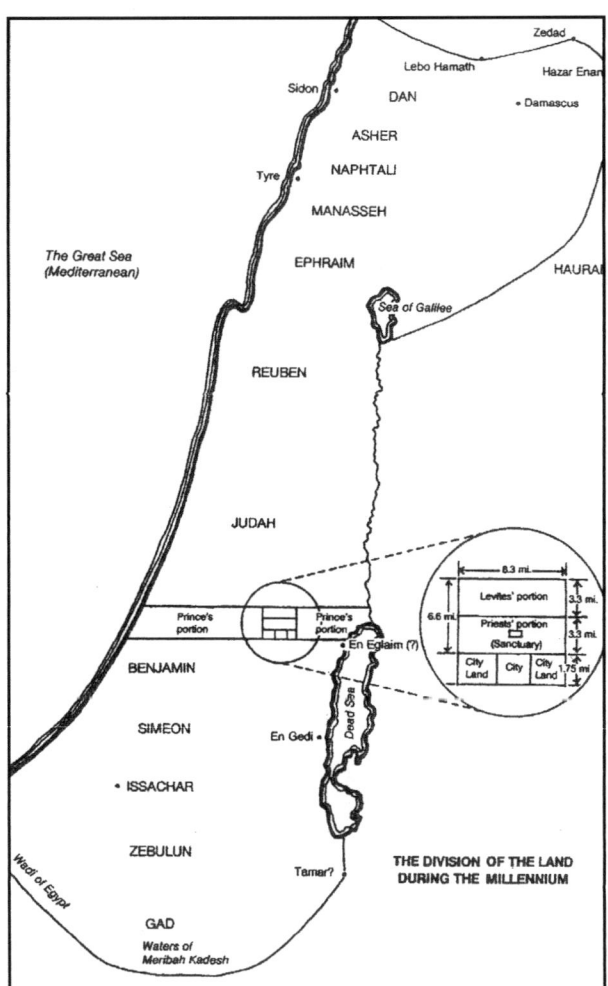

Permission Pending ©2002 Map taken from Warren Wiersbe's *The Bible Exposition Commentary, Old Testament Prophets* (p. 242).

## The Lord Is There (Ezekiel 48:30-35)

While the outer and inner courts of the new temple each had three entrances, the city itself, which would surround the temple, would have twelve gates. Each gate was named after one of the twelve sons of Israel, with Joseph's name (in place of Ephraim's and Manasseh's) returned to its proper place among his brothers. The perimeter of the city would be about 5 1/2 miles, but the most glorious thing about it, is its name:

***"THE LORD IS THERE!"***

## Closing Comments

For all the **trepidation** with which most students began this study, there has been a satisfying pay-off: the writings of Ezekiel **can** be understood by conscientious students of the Bible! Apart from the commonly heard allusions to the scary four-faced cherubim transporting the throne of God in chapter one or the mysterious forces of Gog of Magog in chapters thirty-eight and thirty-nine, most of the text of Ezekiel has probably gone unstudied and unappreciated by the majority of Christians. But those who have persevered have certainly gleaned some grand truths!

1. God is not finished with His people Israel. They have been and, to some degree, still are being chastised for unbelief, but they have not been abandoned. Every promise to regather and bless them will be fulfilled.

2. No matter where God's people find themselves, *"The Lord Is There!"* At the book's opening, hundreds of miles away from Jerusalem and five years into the exile, Ezekiel saw the glory of God come right to where he was. Spanning time and space has never been a problem for Israel's God. At the end of the book, twenty-five years into the seventy years of their exile, God still comforted Ezekiel with His presence and trusted him with His plans for the far-off future. Our comfort today still comes directly from His personal presence and His anointed word, wherever we are.

3. Sometimes we have to wait for God to fulfill His will. While Ezekiel was trusted with the visions of a promisingly glorious future for His people, he did not live to see it come to pass. Nevertheless, he did not shirk the responsibility he had been given to take part in the chain of events that would one day bring it all to complete fulfillment. His responsibility was to stand as a watchman and warn the people in his charge. Are we willing to serve faithfully in that position while we wait for God to make all things right for His people at last? Are we content to lead others to a true relationship and watch them go on in His blessings while we serve faithfully where He has placed us? God is still searching for men and women who will stand in the gap for His people. Will we follow the example of our now beloved brother Ezekiel? Let it be so.

## VOCABULARY

1. **ecclesiastical:** religious, as opposed to secular
2. **ornate:** decorated, having ornamentation
3. **trepidation:** great fear or dread

# Notes

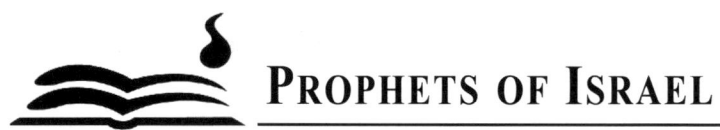

# PROPHETS OF ISRAEL — LESSON 16

## Daily Bible Study Questions

**Study Procedure:** Read the Scripture references before answering questions. Unless otherwise instructed, use the Bible only in answering questions. Some questions may be more difficult than others but try to answer as many as you can. Pray for God's wisdom and understanding as you study and don't be discouraged if some answers are not obvious at first.

**THIS WEEK'S MEMORY VERSE:**

(Daniel 2:20,21) *"...Blessed be the name of God forever and ever, for wisdom and might are His. And He changes the times and the seasons; He removes kings and raises up kings; He gives wisdom to the wise and knowledge to those who have understanding."*

**FIRST DAY: Review of Ezekiel 40-48; Read Daniel 1:1-7**

1. List as many reasons as you can for the vision of a rebuilt Jerusalem and a new temple being given to Ezekiel to be recorded for his people.

2. If this is to be accepted as a prophecy of a literal city and temple, at what time-period could we expect it to exist? Support your answer.

3. Think back over your study of the book of Ezekiel. Describe at least one vision Ezekiel received or one prophetic role-playing activity in which he participated that you found especially interesting or memorable.

4. Read Daniel 1:1-7. In 605 B.C., Babylon's Nebuchadnezzar successfully besieged King Jehoiakim's Jerusalem. However, who did Scripture indicate was really behind Judah's fall to Babylon?

5. What particular objects and persons were brought to Babylon from Judah and for what purpose(s)?

   (a) objects

   (b) persons

Page 59

# LESSON 16

PROPHETS OF ISRAEL

## SECOND DAY: Read Daniel 1:8-21

6. Read Isaiah 39 about an incident that happened a hundred years prior to the first besieging of Judah by Babylon.
   (a) How was Isaiah's prophecy fulfilled in what was happening in Daniel 1?

   (b) What might that prophecy indicate about the lineage of Daniel and his friends and any initial treatment they might have received?

7. What were the plans for assimilating the young men into Babylonian culture?

8. Since Daniel did seem to accept the re-education and renaming enforced by his captors,
   (a) why do you think he *"purposed in his heart"* not to follow the proposed eating arrangements as well?

   (b) What indication was there that God approved of his decision?

9. As a lesson in tact and diplomacy, outline Daniel's method for gaining permission for himself and his friends to follow their own eating plan. Comment on what you learn from this.

10. What were the short-term and long-term results of the young men's determination to follow this plan?
    (a) short-term

    (b) long-term

Page 60

# LESSON 16 — PROPHETS OF ISRAEL

## THIRD DAY: Read Daniel 2

11. Read Daniel 2:1-13. Early in his reign, Nebuchadnezzar, king of Babylon, was troubled by a strange dream and so assembled his staff of spiritual advisers to help him understand it.
    (a) What did he command them to do?

    (b) Why did they not comply?

12. Read Daniel 2:14-18. What bold action did Daniel take when he and his companions were sought out to be killed with the other wise men?

13. Read Daniel 2:19-23, giving special attention to his prayer. What can you learn from this?

14. Read Daniel 2:24-28. Although Arioch, the royal executioner, took credit for bringing Daniel to Nebuchadnezzar to interpret the dream, to whom did Daniel give all the credit for revealing the secrets he was about to explain?

15. Read the details of the dream in Daniel 2:29-45 and fill in the blanks on the chart that follows about the succession of future world powers.

| | Body Part | Material | Name of Country |
|---|---|---|---|
| (a) | Head | _____ | _____ (Daniel 2:37,38) |
| (b) | _____ | Silver | _____ (Daniel 5:28) |
| (c) | _____ | _____ | Greece |
| (d) | _____ | _____ | Rome |
| (e) | _____ | _____ | Extension of original Roman Empire |

©1918 Clarence Larkin

Page 61

# LESSON 16
**PROPHETS OF ISRAEL**

## FOURTH DAY: Continue in Daniel 2

16. What new kingdom was symbolized by the stone "cut without hands" that struck and then crushed the image? (See Psalm 118:22, Isaiah 28:16, and Mark 12:10-12.)

17. What truths do you suppose God wanted to communicate to the following people by revealing these future changes in world power?
    (a) to Nebuchadnezzar

    (b) to Daniel and his people

18. Read Daniel 2:46-49. What all did Nebuchadnezzar do in response to this interpretation of his dream?
    (a) personally

    (b) for Danicl

    (c) for Daniel's friends

## FIFTH DAY: Read Daniel 3

19. Read Daniel 3:1-7. Considering the events of Chapter 2, what is interesting about the description of this image?

20. What do you think Nebuchadnezzar was trying to accomplish?

Page 62

# LESSON 16 — PROPHETS OF ISRAEL

21. Read Daniel 3:8-18. The Jewish trio of Shadrach, Meshach, and Abed-Nego were quickly turned in for refusing to worship the image. How did they respond to the king's offer of a second chance to bow to the image?

22. Read Daniel 3:19-30. What evidences of the miraculous were present in their deliverance out of their furnace of judgment?

23. What was Nebuchadnezzar's response to the miracle?

24. From what you have studied so far in Daniel, what would you say is the main theme or purpose of this book?

# Notes

## DANIEL 1-3

### Starring Role

Center-stage, throughout the whole Old Testament, was the nation of Israel. Other nations were treated like supporting actors in the continuing world-saga, entering and exiting the stage of history, only to interact with Israel under the careful direction of the Most High God. At the beginning of Daniel's exile (605 B.C.), God had begun to remove Israel to the wings of the world-stage for a time, because of her persistent rebellion against His clear directions. Daniel was chosen to receive and record the future plan for the movement of other nations in the world's theater until the time when God would return Israel to international prominence in the latter days of history.

Much like the sacred temple vessels taken from Jerusalem to be proudly displayed as trophies in Babylon, Daniel and his friends were transported to the palace of Babylon to enhance the court-life there. They would become marvelous examples of what every Israelite had been meant to be: holy human vessels, filled with God's Spirit, ready to lead the people of the world by word and action to the knowledge of the Most High God.

These young teen-age captives were examples of the righteous remnant God had promised to preserve until such a time when their whole nation would return to Him in whole-hearted repentance. Away from everything familiar, apart from any who would hold them accountable, they chose to stand fast in the faith of their fathers, to become a minority voice among a very wicked majority. The pages of Daniel's book gloriously recorded the huge impact their consistent righteousness had on the world around them.

The **sovereignty** of God over all the affairs of men as well as the power available through a single person completely committed to God are the twin themes of the book of Daniel. Tracing both through this study should comfort, encourage, and challenge us all.

### The History (Daniel 1:1,2)

Just as Isaiah had prophesied to King Hezekiah in Isaiah 39 a hundred years before, the Babylonian takeover of Judah began in 605 B.C. The fall of Judah would occur in three stages. The first stage was recorded by Daniel and included his being taken among the exiles of Judah to Babylon. Earlier that year, Babylon had successfully defeated Egypt at the battle of Carchemish on the upper Euphrates River. For a few years prior to that time, Egypt had exercised some control over Judah, but after this defeat, Judah was left without this ally, vulnerable to the expansion program of Babylon. Nebuchadnezzar organized a **siege** on Jerusalem which resulted in King Jehoiakim being removed from the throne and bound for **deportation** to Babylon, along with the special vessels used in temple worship, and some of the choice young men of the kingdom. (See 2 Kings 24:1-5 and 2 Chronicles 36:5-7 for more information.) Nebuchadnezzar was interrupted in his takeover efforts by news of the death of his father Nabopolasser and had to leave Jerusalem and return quickly to Babylon to claim the throne. He would lead two more attacks on Jerusalem, the next in 597 when Ezekiel was taken captive, and the last, which brought about the final destruction of the city, in 587-586 B.C.

### Assimilation (Daniel 1:3-20)

Nebuchadnezzar had a plan to profit fully from his conquests. Before returning to claim his throne, he instructed Ashpenaz, the master of his eunuchs, to select the best young men from Israel, particularly from among the king's heirs and noblemen, to be transported to Babylon to enter a three-year re-education program through which they could learn the language and literature of his country and become useful advisors in the affairs of state. The custom of making high-ranking officials into eunuchs helped insure that they would be motivated to serve the king without being tempted to promote their own personal plans for establishing a dynasty. If this were enforced on Daniel and his friends, as alluded to in Isaiah 39, as indicated by the titles given to the men in charge of them (Daniel 1:9), and

# LESSON 16

by the absence of any mention of wives or children in the account of their lives, how much more amazing their faithfulness to God stands out in this record.

As part of the plan to assimilate them fully into Babylonian culture, the four young men had their names changed from compounds which included *Jah* or *El,* in honor of their God Jehovah, sometimes called *Elohim,* to compounds which included the names of the Babylonian gods *Bel, Aku,* and *Nebo.* In addition to this, they were intensively trained in all the wisdom and literature of the ruling class in Babylon called the Chaldeans. The Chaldeans had been a recognized group in the twelfth and eleventh centuries B.C. around the Persian Gulf before Babylon's rise to world dominance and subsequently became the leaders of that nation. As such, they were frequently referred to as the wise men of that land.

Another component of Daniel and his friends' assimilation into Babylonian court-life was the provision of rich foods from the king's own table. However, it was this "perk" that the young men refused to receive. Why make an issue over food? Daniel did not detail his reasons in this instance, but from knowledge of Scripture one can assume it had to do with these issues: First, accepting food from another in fellowship was seen as a covenant act, an action of approval that showed a willingness to be identified with them in their faith or a desire to be joined with them in their life. These young men were not willing to make that commitment. Also, Israel had been given a strict eating-plan from God, not only to keep them healthy but also to make them distinct among the pagans. This plan banned the eating of blood, pork, or other unclean foods; heathen cultures recognized no such restrictions. Further, the Babylonian delicacies may have also been used first as offerings to idols, which Daniel and his friends might have found offensive. Which ever the reason, God's Spirit was leading Daniel, and he *"purposed in his heart"* not to participate in the proposed food-plan.

As a model of tact and politeness, Daniel approached the chief of the eunuchs, who was in charge of the larger group, with his request. While God had granted favor to Daniel in this man's sight, the officer did not want to take responsibility for the young men's disobedience to the king's direct orders and the possibility of their becoming sickly as a result. Daniel did not give up, however, and appealed to the steward, who was more personally involved with their care. Maybe because he might keep the rich food for himself or maybe just because he recognized God's hand on Daniel, the steward agreed to Daniel's request for a trial period of ten days. Not only at the end of the ten days but also at the end of the entire training period, Daniel and his friends were judged by Nebuchadnezzar as being *"ten times better than all the magicians and astrologers who were in all his realm"* (Daniel 1:20). Daniel's personal excellence and righteousness in all activities would keep him in active service for the next sixty years, up to and beyond the time King Cyrus of Persia conquered Babylon in 539 B.C. God sooner or later always blesses those who obey His leading.

## Nebuchadnezzar's Dream (Daniel 2:1-24)

The next two chapters detailed God's personal dealings with a pagan king. The record emphasized God's role in the affairs of men: He is in charge; kings and kingdoms rise and fall at His direction. Foolish are the leaders or the nations who fail to realize that they serve only at His pleasure. Nebuchadnezzar was to be educated in these truths.

God's first lesson for Nebuchadnezzar began with a dream which interrupted his royal sleep and caused him great alarm. He called for the magicians, astrologers, sorcerers, and Chaldeans on his payroll to assemble and interpret the dream; for some reason, Daniel and his friends were not summoned. Nebuchadnezzar added quite a degree of difficulty to this task, when he demanded that they first retell to him the dream he had received. This certainly helped insure against **fraud**, but according to a phrase included only in the King James Version of Daniel 2:5, Nebuchadnezzar actually admitted, *"The thing is gone from me."* He was so determined to be told the dream and its interpretation that he promised immediate and brutal execution of all who failed, followed by the destruction of all their property. Rewards were promised for any who succeeded.

The Chaldeans responded with what they believed to be true: *"It is a difficult thing that the king requests, and there is no other who can tell it to the king except the gods, whose dwelling is not with flesh"* (Daniel 2:11). With all their education, they had failed to get true wisdom. The God of Creation does dwell with flesh, and at that very moment He was present with Daniel. However, unaware of that, the furious king ordered the executions to begin.

While gathering up the victims, the executioner sought out Daniel and his friends. Daniel asked the captain of the king's guard for the details about what was happening and then boldly approached Nebuchadnezzar himself to ask for time to prepare an interpretation. Having received the time, Daniel gathered his three friends about him and sought God's mercies to reveal the secrets of the king's dream and to spare them personally from execution. God answered by giving Daniel his own vision of the dream, and Daniel responded with a wonderful hymn of praise, recognizing that God removes and raises up kings and dispenses wisdom to the righteous as He wills.

## Daniel's Response (Daniel 2:24-45)

Daniel approached Arioch, the king's appointed executioner, and asked him to stop the killing of the wise men and take him to the king. Taking credit for finding an interpreter of dreams, Arioch presented Daniel to the king. Nebuchadnezzar asked Daniel if he were able to give the dream and its interpretation. Daniel humbly responded by saying only God could reveal such information and had done so for the king, as Daniel would explain.

First of all, Daniel declared, the dream had been given to Nebuchadnezzar to inform him of the future, of occurrences in the *"latter days"* (Daniel 2:28). In just a few sentences, Daniel accurately described the splendid image the king had seen in his dream: *"...head was of fine gold, its chest and arms of silver, its belly and thighs of bronze, its legs of iron, its feet partly of iron and partly of clay"* (Daniel 2:32,33). The dream ended with this scene: a supernaturally cut stone striking the feet of the image, breaking them to pieces. After this, the stone crushed the rest of the image into such fine particles that the wind blew them away completely. The stone then grew into a great mountain that filled the earth.

Daniel's interpretation began on a positive note. He explained that Nebuchadnezzar was the head of gold, which signified his position as king of kings, a place given to him by the God of heaven whom Daniel served. However, after Nebuchadnezzar would rise another kingdom, inferior to Babylon as silver to gold, and then another, represented by the bronze parts of the image, to rule over the earth after him. The fourth kingdom, strong as iron but less glorious than gold, silver, or bronze, would succeed those. The feet and toes of clay mixed with iron symbolized the division in that kingdom which would occur at some point when it would become partly strong and partly fragile. In the days of the kings of that final divided kingdom of iron and clay, God would establish His eternal kingdom, which like the mysterious stone, would break up all the other kingdoms and fill the earth.

When Daniel interpreted this dream, the events were all set in the future. But now, more than twenty-five hundred years later, we can check history and marvel at the absolute accuracy of the prophecy. Babylon was identified as the first kingdom to exercise world dominance in that timeframe. It was to be followed by the chest and arms of silver, which according to another prophecy in Daniel 5:28 was the empire of the Medes and the Persians. From history the identity of the last two can be made. Greece conquered the Medo-Persian Empire to be in turn conquered by the Romans. The Roman empire divided into individual nations, most of which are still recognizable as part of what we know today as Europe. During a time in which those identifiable units are still in existence, God will come to set up His eternal kingdom. That part of the dream still awaits future fulfillment.

Nebuchadnezzar was so thrilled to have the mystery explained, and probably relieved that it promised no real trouble in his lifetime, that he ordered incense, offerings, and gifts to be presented to Daniel and promoted him to the position of ruler of all Babylon and chief administrator over all the wise men. At Daniel's request, the king also promoted Shadrach, Meshach, and Abed-Nego to high positions.

## Critics Attack Daniel

Students of Daniel need to be warned that there has been much published criticism of the book of Daniel specifically because it is so unerringly accurate in its prophecies of the future. Most of what Daniel prophesied can already be verified by searching historical records. That seems to be the problem. Skeptical commentators cannot accept that God would tell Daniel all these details before they happened. They claim that the material in Daniel must have been written by someone other than Daniel after these big events had already occurred. Such scholars just cannot accept the main message of Daniel—God is God and can do what He pleases. Amos stated in our earlier study, *"Surely the Lord GOD does nothing, unless He reveals His secret to His servants the prophets"* (Amos 3:7), and Daniel himself acknowledged: *"For wisdom and might are His....He removes kings and raises up kings; He gives wisdom to the wise and knowledge to those who have understanding. He reveals deep and secret things; He knows what is in the darkness, and light dwells with Him"* (Daniel 2:20-22). Those who deny the power of God to predict the future are really doubting the ability of God to do anything. Despite their objections, God will always be God, omnipotent, omniscient, and omnipresent. His word is true despite their attacks on it or on its authors.

## Fighting the Future (Daniel 3)

Nebuchadnezzar's recognition of the superiority of Daniel's God did not keep him from trying to change what he had been told about the future of his kingdom. In the dream, he had been the head of gold, the king of kings, but in this chapter he evidently decided to go for more; he did not want his vast holdings to be taken over by another kingdom. So he depicted himself through a totally gold image, as irreplaceable king of the world. As defiant as the people of Babel had been in building their tower to heaven, Nebuchadnezzar ordered the construction of a ten-story totem-pole-like image of himself, covered in gold. He gave orders to the assembled officials of his country that all should bow down to the image, whenever the royal orchestra began to play. Quickly the king was alerted to the failure of Shadrach, Meshach, and Abed-Nego to do so. In the unexplained absence of Daniel, they had still taken a bold stand against the idolatry so clearly prohibited by their Jewish law.

Nebuchadnezzar, in a rage, commanded that they be brought to him. He confronted them with one last choice: worship or die. Showing clearly that he had not absorbed the full meaning of the earlier dream from God to him, Nebuchadnezzar pompously challenged, *"And who is the god who will deliver you from my hands?"*

With a courage that only God can give His people in life-or-death situations, the three men assured the king that their God was well able to deliver them from the furnace and out of the king's own hand. Yet, they clarified, if He chose not to do so, they still would not bow down to the golden idol. Even more furious at that response, Nebuchadnezzar ordered the already-burning furnace heated seven times hotter, then had the three men bound and cast into the flames. Those putting them in were themselves killed by the fire, but the three young men fell to the bottom unhurt, set free from their bonds. The construction of the furnace somehow allowed for viewing inside, and Nebuchadnezzar was astonished to see not three, but four men, unbound and walking in the middle of the flames. The fourth, he claimed, was *"like the Son of God."* He called for these servants of *"the Most High God"* to come out. All of the gathered officials witnessed the incredible scene. There was no sign of fire on them: their hair was not singed, their garments were not charred, and they did not even smell like smoke! Nebuchadnezzar burst into praise for their God who had sent His Angel to deliver the men who had trusted in Him. In the face of death, they had still chosen to worship only their own God. (Note: The appearance of the Angel of the Lord or someone described as the Son of God in the Old Testament is called a theophany, or **pre-incarnate** appearance of Jesus.) Nebuchadnezzar decreed that any who spoke against their God would be *"cut in pieces"* and have their houses burned. Then, once again, he promoted the three brave men to higher positions in his kingdom.

# LESSON 16 — PROPHETS OF ISRAEL

## How Much Does It Take?

These three marvelous chapters detailed the way godly young men chose to obey God in spite of the cost or danger and are favorites of millions of Bible readers. God's mercy in giving not one, but two clear demonstrations of His sovereignty to a pagan king must also be applauded. However, the thrilling testimony to the power of the Most High God would soon die from the lips of Babylon's king as he continued to prosper in what he thought to be his own successes at world rule. He would forget God, but God would not forget him. At a terrible cost, in the chapter that follows, Nebuchadnezzar would finally learn, but shame and suffering would come to him first.

How much does it take for you to be completely convinced of the rightful place of God in your life? Refuse to let profound encounters with the Lord fade to shadowy memories. Remember where, when, and how you have been met by God. Repeat the stories and recommit yourself to being a faithful servant whom He will not only rescue in time of trouble but will also find worthy to promote to places of godly leadership for His purposes.

---

### VOCABULARY

1. **deportation:** an act of expelling from a country; banishment
2. **fraud:** willful deceit; deception
3. **pre-incarnate:** before being embodied in flesh
4. **siege:** the act of surrounding any fortified place with the intention of capturing it
5. **sovereignty:** supreme authority

# Notes

# Notes

# PROPHETS OF ISRAEL

## LESSON 17

## Daily Bible Study Questions

**Study Procedure:** Read the Scripture references before answering questions. Unless otherwise instructed, use the Bible only in answering questions. Some questions may be more difficult than others but try to answer as many as you can. Pray for God's wisdom and understanding as you study and don't be discouraged if some answers are not obvious at first.

### THIS WEEK'S MEMORY VERSE:

(Daniel 5:23b) *"...And you have praised the gods of silver and gold, bronze and iron, wood and stone, which do not see or hear or know; and the God who holds your breath in His hand and owns all your ways, you have not glorified."*

### FIRST DAY: Review of Daniel 1-3

1. Multiple choice:
    (a) He was king of Judah when Daniel and friends were deported.
       1. Jehoiakim    2. Jehoiachin    3. Hezekiah

    (b) This was what Nebuchadnezzar did to conquer Jerusalem.
       1. burned it    2. besieged it    3. flooded it

    (c) This was not listed as part of the assimilation process for the Jewish exiles in Nebuchadnezzar's court.
       1. giving them Babylonian names
       2. providing them food from the king's table
       3. giving them Babylonian wives
       4. teaching them from the wisdom and literature of the Chaldeans

    (d) Daniel stayed in public service in Babylon for this many years.
       1. twenty years    2. forty years    3. sixty years

    (e) The dream Daniel interpreted in chapter two had to do with this.
       1. the future succession of world powers
       2. the decline in value of precious metals
       3. the dangers of idolatry

    (f) For their courage in refusing to worship the golden image, Shadrach, Meshech, and Abed-Nego experienced this.
       1. a visit from one *"like the Son of God"*
       2. protection from the fire and smoke of the furnace
       3. a promotion to better jobs

# LESSON 17

**PROPHETS OF ISRAEL**

2. What new, challenging, or inspiring information did you glean from last week's lesson?

**SECOND DAY: Read Daniel 4**

3. Read all of Daniel 4, which is Nebuchadnezzar's own account of how the Most High God finally convinced him to humble himself and acknowledge His authority. Matching.

    _____(a) Where was Nebuchadnezzar when he had this dream?
    _____(b) What, according to Nebuchadnezzar, made Daniel different from the other wise men in his court?
    _____(c) What in the dream reached to heaven, could be seen from all over the earth, and provided food and shelter for all men and beasts?
    _____(d) What was a *"watcher"*?
    _____(e) What orders did the watcher give?
    _____(f) What was this purpose for this?
    _____(g) Daniel was greatly troubled by the dream. Nebuchadnezzar had to encourage him to speak. To whom did Daniel wish that the dream applied?
    _____(h) Whom did the tree represent?
    _____(i) What was going to happen to Nebuchadnezzar?
    _____(j) What did Daniel urge him to do that might cause God to lengthen his time of prosperity?
    _____(k) How long was it before the vision came to pass?
    _____(l) What was the ultimate result in the life of Nebuchadnezzar?

1. an angel
2. in him was the Spirit of the Holy God
3. twelve months
4. a great tree
5. Nebuchadnezzar
6. He acknowledged God as the Most High and praised and worshiped Him.
7. to cut down the tree and its branches, strip its leaves, scatter its fruit, but to save the stump and roots
8. to replace sin with righteousness, showing mercy to the poor
9. "...that the living may know that the Most High rules in the kingdom of men, gives it to whomever He will, and sets over it the lowest of men."
10. in his house in his palace
11. to Nebuchadnezzar's enemies
12. He would be driven from men and would live with beasts, acting like an animal for seven times (years) until he acknowledged that the Most High rules the world and chooses men to rule.

Page 72

# LESSON 17 — PROPHETS OF ISRAEL

4. Comment on anything you found interesting or meaningful from Nebuchadnezzar's testimony in Chapter 4.

## THIRD DAY: Read Daniel 5

**Historical Note:** King Nebuchadnezzar died on October 7, 562 B.C. and was succeeded by three other men who served briefly and passed from the historical record. After that, Nabonidus, son of Nebuchadnezzar, assumed the throne in 556 B.C., but after traveling westward to put down a distant revolt against Babylonian control, he built and lived in a palace at Tema, in the Arabian peninsula, and stayed away from Babylon for about ten years. During his absence, his son Belshazzar ruled in his place.

5. Read Daniel 5:1-4. Belshazzar would have been old enough to know about the God of Israel's dealings with his grandfather Nebuchadnezzar. Why do you think he chose to publicly desecrate the temple vessels at this time by using them at the drunken feast he was hosting?

6. Read Daniel 5:5-9. What was Belshazzar's reaction to the handwriting on the wall?

7. Read Daniel 5:10-12. What help did the queen offer?

8. Read Daniel 5:13-23. Summarize a few of the main points Daniel made to Belshazzar before he interpreted the mysterious handwriting on the wall.

9. Read Daniel 5:24-30. Give Daniel's interpretation for these words.
   (a) *Mene*

   (b) *Tekel*

   (c) *Upharsin* (literally "half-shekels" from the root word of *peres*)

# LESSON 17    PROPHETS OF ISRAEL

10. How was the prophecy fulfilled that very night?

**FOURTH DAY: Read Daniel 6**

11. Read Daniel 6:1-3. Darius the Mede, the conqueror of Babylon, recognized the *"excellent spirit"* in Daniel and allowed him to continue in leadership. What were Daniel's new responsibilities?

12. Read Daniel 6:4-9. Not surprisingly, many were jealous of Daniel and plotted to bring him down. What did they invent to bring this about?

13. Read Daniel 6:10-23. With full awareness of the new law, Daniel continued in his regular prayer routine.
    (a) What was the king's response when Daniel's disobedience to the new law was brought to his attention?

    (b) What all did the king do that revealed his great affection for Daniel and respect for Daniel's God?

14. Read Daniel 6:24-28. After Daniel's deliverance, what else happened to confirm that his safety had been a real miracle of God?

15. What occurred again on a national level because of the bold faith of Daniel in this incident?

# LESSON 17
**PROPHETS OF ISRAEL**

**FIFTH DAY: Read Daniel 7:1-10**

16. Read Daniel 7:1,2. Jumping back in time, Daniel 7 described a dream and visions Daniel received in the first year of Belshazzar's reign as ruler in Babylon. Paralleling Nebuchadnezzar's earlier dream of the multi-metaled image, the symbols for each succeeding Gentile nation in this vision were depicted by wild animals. Consult a map of the Middle East. What was the identity of the Great Sea of verse 2?

17. Read Daniel 7:3-8. Out of the Great Sea came four vicious beasts. Describe them below.
    (a) 1st animal:

    (b) How did its description fit in with what you know about the life of Nebuchadnezzar?

    (c) 2nd animal:

    (d) Other characteristics:

    (e) 3rd animal:

    (f) Other characteristics:

    (g) 4th animal:

    (h) Other characteristics:

    (i) What details included about this fourth beast would correspond to the description of the kingdom of iron and clay represented by the feet and toes of the image in Nebuchadnezzar's dream of chapter two?

Page 75

# LESSON 17  PROPHETS OF ISRAEL

18. Read Daniel 7:9,10. If the theme of the book of Daniel is the sovereignty of God, how does this scene emphasize it? (See also Revelation 1:13 and 5:11.)

19. Read Daniel 7:11,12.
    (a) What happened to the pompous speaking horn on the fourth beast?

    (b) What happened to the other beasts?

20. Who is described in Daniel 7:13,14? Give proof for your answer from Scripture. (See Mark 14:61,62 and Revelation 1:4-7.)

21. Why do you think the Holy Spirit had these verses (9-14) precede the interpretation of the terrible fourth beast which will follow in our next lesson?

# Notes

## DANIEL 4:1-7:14

### New Author (Daniel 4:1-18)

This chapter, written by Nebuchadnezzar himself, began with a proclamation to the whole world, announcing his purpose: *"I thought it good to declare the signs and wonders that the Most High God has worked for me."* Before he began his story, he eased the minds of his hearers by indicating they would experience a happy ending. That is still an effective way to encourage a listener to sit still for a strange story. And strange this was!

The Lord, still showing mercy in reaching out to this pagan king, sent him another dream. As before, Nebuchadnezzar first called for the magicians, Chaldeans, astrologers, and soothsayers for an interpretation, but they were unable to help him. Then he called Daniel, who listened as the king recounted the visions. The king dreamed that a huge tree in the middle of the earth grew to heaven, visible to the whole world and loaded with lush growth and abundant fruit. From it, all creatures were nourished and under it all were sheltered. A *"watcher"* or *"holy one"* from heaven came down with orders to chop it down, cut its branches, strip its leaves, scatter its fruit, and bind its roots and stump with metal bands. Then the angel's terminology changed from *"let it be wet"* to *"let him graze with the beasts,"* and the vision suddenly became quite personal for the king (Daniel 4:15). The order was given to change the king's heart to that of a beast for a period of seven *"times,"* most probably years, and then the *"watcher"* announced the reason for such a harsh sentence: it was so *"that the living may know that the Most High rules in the kingdom of men, gives it to whomever He will, and sets over it the lowest of men."*

### The Interpretation (Daniel 4:19-37)

Daniel was astonished and troubled by the dream. Nebuchadnezzar tried to comfort him, but Daniel voiced his anxiety about the interpretation by wishing aloud, *"My lord, may the dream concern...your enemies!"* (Daniel 4:19). Then he began his explanation.

The tree reaching to heaven was Nebuchadnezzar and the descriptive details emphasized his current *"dominion to the end of the earth."* The watcher's call for the cutting down of the tree except for stump and roots and the changing of the king into some sort of being content to dwell with beasts of the field would come to pass. The king would be driven from the company of men and somehow caused to eat grass like an ox, enduring the dew of heaven in the open fields. This would continue for a specified period until he came to the point of acknowledging that the Most High God rules as He sees fit. Whether caused by an evil spirit or diagnosed as a recognizable mental illness, the king would be out of office, but his kingdom would still be waiting for him when he recovered.

With the interpretation at an end, Daniel pleaded with his beloved sovereign: *"Break off your sins by being righteous, and your iniquities by showing mercy to the poor. Perhaps there may be a lengthening of your prosperity"* (Daniel 4:27).

The king obviously did not take Daniel's advice or heed the words of the watcher in the dream who told clearly of God's requirement that Nebuchadnezzar humble himself and recognize His supremacy. Just twelve months later, with self-glorifying words still on his lips, Nebuchadnezzar heard a voice from heaven announce to him: *"King Nebuchadnezzar,...the kingdom has departed from you!"* (Daniel 4:31). That very same hour, the madness fell on the king. The dream was fulfilled as he was cast out as a beast and took on the characteristics of a wild animal, complete with hair *"like eagles' feathers and his nails like birds' claws."*

After the time was completed, his understanding returned, and he did glorify God as the true holder of power and eternal dominion. The happy ending was reiterated in the final verse, *"Now I, Nebuchadnezzar, praise and extol and honor the King of heaven, all of whose works are truth, and His ways justice. And those who walk in pride He is able to cut down"* (Daniel 4:37). That king had learned it all the hard way, but imagine what stories he would be able to tell to the saints in heaven!

## Belshazzar's Bold Defiance (Daniel 5:1-4)

Years after Nebuchadnezzar's death, his grandson Belshazzar was appointed acting king, while his father Nabonidus was away for ten years in Arabia. Belshazzar was a teenager when Nebuchadnezzar died and would have known first hand about the Most High God's dealings with his grandfather. However, in mockery of his grandfather's reverence for the God of Israel and in direct defiance of the prophetic warnings that the Babylonian kingdom would fall to the Medes and the Persians, Belshazzar brought out the temple vessels from Jerusalem to be used by his guests at the drunken orgy he hosted for a thousand people, while the Medes and the Persians were setting up a siege outside the city walls. The officials of Babylon thought their capital, with its gigantic walls, was indestructible. Many living in surrounding cities recently conquered by the Medes and the Persians had sought refuge within the city walls, assured of continuous fresh water from the River Euphrates which flowed under the city and a supply of food stores estimated to last them twenty years. However, as Nebuchadnezzar had announced in Daniel 4:37, God is able to put down those who walk in pride, and in the case of Belshazzar, He would do it suddenly. Belshazzar's arrogance provided God with another way to demonstrate His sovereignty in the affairs of men.

## God's Response (Daniel 5:5-31)

In the same hour that Belshazzar had the temple vessels brought out for his guests, while the king watched in terror, the fingers of a man's hand supernaturally appeared to write something on the wall of the palace. In keeping with their pattern of failure in discerning the workings of God, the assembled wise men could not interpret the writing. The queen heard the commotion, came to the banquet hall, and respectfully suggested that Daniel be called. She reviewed his history of helping Nebuchadnezzar and pointed out that in him was the *"Spirit of the Holy God"* (Daniel 5:11).

When Daniel arrived, the obvious warmth with which he had always addressed Nebuchadnezzar was absent. He was polite but cool to Belshazzar, refusing the offer to become third ruler of Babylon while agreeing to give the interpretation of the writing. Daniel began with a review of Nebuchadnezzar's association with the Most High God and his subsequent acknowledgment of God's sovereignty. He chastised Belshazzar for ignoring these facts, for refusing to humble himself before the true God (Daniel 5:22), and for toasting false gods with sacred vessels while disregarding the God who allowed him to take each breath. That God, the true God, had sent the fingers to write the message which spelled doom for the nation:

*"MENE: God has numbered your kingdom, and finished it;*

*TEKEL: You have been weighed in the balances, and found wanting;*

*PERES: Your kingdom has been divided, and given to the Medes and Persians."*

While Belshazzar kept his word and promoted Daniel to third ruler, the honor was short-lived. That very night the Medes and Persians, led by Darius the Mede, diverted the river away from the city, walked through the empty waterways under the city walls, and conquered the city. Belshazzar was slain that same night, October 13, 539 B.C. So much for shaking a puny fist at the Most High God and ignoring His prophetic warnings!

## Where's Cyrus?

Daniel referred to the conqueror of Babylon as Darius the Mede. However the Persian king Cyrus was credited by historians with conquering Babylon in 539 B.C. and allowing the Jewish exiles to return to Israel. The dispute may be settled either by accepting that Darius the Mede was Cyrus' vassal-king or by accepting the work of some linguists who claim that "Darius" was a title and not a proper name, so that the title could be referring to Cyrus. There are other proposed solutions as well, but the dilemma has not been completely settled. Aware of the controversy, we will use the names Daniel has given us.

## Evil Efforts by Jealous Leaders (Daniel 6)

Chapter six began with Darius organizing his newly acquired kingdom under three governors, with Daniel being chosen to serve as one of them. Daniel did such an excellent job that Darius was considering the idea of promoting him to chief executive over the whole realm (Daniel 6:3). Word of this immediately stirred up jealousy among the other governors and satraps. They hurried to find some way to discredit Daniel but could not. The only possibility they found was if the laws of their land could be made to conflict with the laws of his God. In that case, they knew where his loyalty would lie. This they accomplished by flattering Darius into signing a royal statute forbidding any person from asking anyone other than Darius—that included requests to God or man—for anything for thirty days.

Daniel heard of the law being signed, knew what they intended to accomplish with it, but went right ahead with his regular prayers to God anyway. His enemies assembled to find him in the act of praying and quickly told the king about Daniel's disobedience. Evidently Darius cared greatly for Daniel because he was grieved that this had happened. However, Darius could find no legally allowable way to undo the law he had signed. So when the men pressed him to throw Daniel to the lions, he reluctantly gave orders to do so, yet not without offering words of hope to his friend: *"Your God, whom you serve continually, He will deliver you"* (Daniel 6:16).

An angel was sent from God to shut the mouths of the hungry lions, and so, while Daniel probably slept that night, Darius did not. He fasted and prayed for Daniel, rising at first light to check on his friend: *"Daniel, servant of the living God, has your God, whom you serve continually, been able to deliver you from the lions?"* To the king's great relief, Daniel answered and assured him that God had found him innocent and had saved his life. Darius had Daniel taken out of the den and had his accusers and their families thrown in. The lions were so fierce and hungry that they crushed the bones of everyone before the bodies even hit the ground! What a miracle of deliverance for Daniel and what an opportunity for yet another king to see the sovereign power of the Most High God!

Daniel's obedience allowed Darius to witness God's power and to declare it publicly to his new nation. God did not spare Daniel from the lion's den but was with him in power in the lion's den. Our sufferings for Christ's sake can be used for God's glory just as Daniel's were, so long as our faith and obedience are exercised in times of trouble. Do your tribulations glorify God?

## Daniel's Vision Introduced

Chapter seven jumps backward in time about eleven or more years to 550 BC., to the first year in which Belshazzar served as Babylon's king. In this lesson Daniel's dream will be introduced, but because of some of the more complicated imagery, the full interpretation will follow in the next lesson.

Many people see in this vision a close parallel to Nebuchadnezzar's dream in chapter two about the succeeding world powers depicted by a multi-metaled image. That dream was said to depict man's view of power—glorious, powerful, and predictable. In contrast, Daniel's dream gives God's view of the progression of human governments and the effects of those governments on Israel—beastly, merciless, and evil.

## The Great Sea and the First Beast (Daniel 7:1-4)

Daniel's dream began with a vision of the four winds of heaven blowing in on the Great Sea—the Mediterranean—and stirring it up. This would signify that whatever was about to happen had world-wide significance. Next four beasts came up from the sea in a recognizable order, each different from the other. The first was like a lion with eagle's wings, but the wings were plucked off while Daniel watched. The creature was then raised up to walk on two feet like a man and given a man's heart.

This and the next two beasts were obviously understood by Daniel, since he did not stop and explain them. Bible and scholars of secular history find the meanings to be clear. Archeologists have found the winged-lion to be a common **motif** in the

**excavations** of Babylon. This beast stood for Nebuchadnezzar, who, at the height of his power, had his "wings" clipped by God with a dose of insanity until he humbled himself and acknowledged that the Most High God was sovereign over even kings and kingdoms. God gave him a new heart to know Him and serve Him. That has generally been accepted as the interpretation of the first beast.

## The Second Beast (Daniel 7:5)

The second was like a bear, with one side a bit higher than the other, holding three ribs between its teeth. It was given orders to *"arise, devour much flesh!"* (Daniel 7:5). Historians parallel this with the kingdom of the Medes and Persians, who, like the shoulders of the bear, were not always seen as equal in power. They overthrew Babylon in 539 B.C. The ribs seem to represent three major conquests which still had not satisfied the beast's ravenous appetite: Egypt, Babylon, and Lydia.

## The Third Beast (Daniel 7:6)

The third beast rising from the Great Sea was a leopard, already legendary for speed, who also had four wings on its back. These wings emphasized even more speed. History recorded that Alexander the Great of Greece amassed great military might and conquered the known world, more than 11,000 miles of territory, in just eight years. He conquered Medo-Persia in 331 B.C. At his death (he was only 32), rivals killed his legitimate heir, an illegitimate heir, and his mentally retarded brother and then divided the vast kingdom among four of his generals. This explains the four heads of the winged leopard Daniel saw.

## The Fourth Beast (Daniel 7:7,8)

The last beast to emerge from the water in Daniel's dream was *"dreadful and terrible, exceedingly strong"* with *"huge iron teeth."* It was so different from what Daniel knew in the natural world that he did not compare it with an existing animal. It was the worst beast of all and had ten horns. A very strange thing happened among the horns while Daniel studied them in his dream. A small horn emerged, displacing three of the original ones. That little horn had eyes like a man and a mouth to speak *"pompous words."* While the mention of iron in the teeth of the beast serves to link this fourth beast to the fourth segment of Nebuchadnezzar's image which was made of iron, further revelation was needed for Daniel to understand all its strange features, especially the talking little horn. That will be investigated in the following lesson.

## Now a Word from Our Sponsor! (Daniel 7:9-14)

This next vision of *"the Ancient of Days"* was most likely given to comfort Daniel and all who would read his words in years to come, that in spite of the beastly nature of future world rulers, God remained firmly on His throne. He rules the universe. At His service are uncountable angelic forces. He is the Judge who alone rules in the world court, and He has ordered the books to be opened.

While Daniel watched God the Father holding court, he was still aware of the little horn's pompous words. However, as he watched, the last beast was slain and its body destroyed by fire. The other beasts had their dominion taken from them, although Daniel understood they would live some time longer.

After the destruction of the last beast and, with it, the silencing of its little horn, Daniel saw one who looked like *"the Son of Man, coming with the clouds of heaven! He came to the Ancient of Days, and they brought Him near before Him. Then to Him was given dominion and glory and a kingdom, that all peoples, nations, and languages should serve Him..."* (Daniel 7:13,14).

Many times in Scripture, this same description was given of the Second Coming of Christ as King of Kings to bring justice and establish righteousness on earth. How important it is to keep both these visions in mind, not only as we proceed to study some of the frightening details of future events but also as we go about our daily duties. No matter what opposition forms against us personally or internationally, the Most High God is on His throne directing all things, and His Son, our Savior, will be the final Victor over all the beastly activities devised by human governments. (For cross-references to these verses see Matthew 24:30; 26:64; Mark 13:26; 14:62; Revelation 1:5-7; 14:14; Psalm 2:6-8.)

## What an Influence!

In reviewing just these chapters we can see what a long-term influence Daniel's godliness had on two kingdoms. He served under three kings, and two were convinced and (hopefully) converted through his influence. Social or political positions pose no threat to the workings of the Most High God. For His purposes and for the sake of His children, He can manipulate nature (lions and fire) or change the hearts of kings. What difficulties should you bring before His throne?

---

### VOCABULARY

1. **excavations:** archeological diggings in which buried artifacts from past cultures are carefully removed
2. **motif:** pattern, repeated decorative theme

# Notes

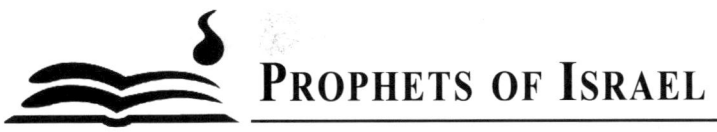

# PROPHETS OF ISRAEL — LESSON 18

## Daily Bible Study Questions

**Study Procedure:** Read the Scripture references before answering questions. Unless otherwise instructed, use the Bible only in answering questions. Some questions may be more difficult than others but try to answer as many as you can. Pray for God's wisdom and understanding as you study and don't be discouraged if some answers are not obvious at first.

**THIS WEEK'S MEMORY VERSE:**

(Daniel 9:24) *"Seventy weeks are determined for your people and for your holy city, to finish the transgression, to make an end of sins, to make reconciliation for iniquity, to bring in everlasting righteousness, to seal up vision and prophecy, and to anoint the Most Holy."*

**FIRST DAY: Review of Daniel 4:1-7:14; Read Daniel 7:15-22**

1. What would you emphasize if asked to teach the following passages?
   (a) Nebuchadnezzar's temporary fall from power (Daniel 4)

   (b) The handwriting on the wall addressed to Belshazzar (Daniel 5)

   (c) The plot against Daniel that landed him in the lions' den (Daniel 6)

   (d) The heavenly throne-room scene in the middle of Daniel's vision of the four beasts (Daniel 7)

2. Read Daniel 7:15-18. In what interesting way did Daniel receive the interpretation of this dream?

Page 83

# LESSON 18  PROPHETS OF ISRAEL

3. Read Daniel 7:19-22. What new information is given here that was not given in the first review of this dream?

**SECOND DAY: Read Daniel 7:23-28**

4. Read Daniel 7:23-25. In the fourth kingdom which differed from the first three and was allowed to devour the whole earth, what did the horns represent?

5. Describe the new king, who rises after the first ten, uprooting three.
   (a) What will he be like?

   (b) What will he intend to do?

   (c) How long will he control the saints?

6. To confirm Daniel's vision, God placed other prophetic warnings in the Bible about a mysterious and dangerous man who will appear in the last days of this world. Read each of the Scriptures below and underline the name or names which reveal the character of this man as well as any other details you find interesting about him.

   (a) (Daniel 7:8) *"I was considering the horns, and there was another horn, a little one, coming up among them, before whom three of the first horns were plucked out by the roots. And there, in this horn, were eyes like the eyes of a man, and a mouth speaking pompous words."*

   (b) (2 Thessalonians 2:3-8) *"Let no one deceive you by any means; for that Day will not come unless the falling away comes first, and the man of sin is revealed, the son of perdition, who opposes and exalts himself above all that is called God or that is worshiped, so that he sits as God in the temple of God, showing himself that he is God. Do you not remember that when I was still with you I told you these things? And now*

Page 84

*you know what is restraining, that he may be revealed in his own time. For the mystery of lawlessness is already at work; only He who now restrains will do so until He is taken out of the way. And then the lawless one will be revealed, whom the Lord will consume with the breath of His mouth and destroy with the brightness of His coming."*

(c) (1 John 2:18) *"Little children, it is the last hour; and as you have heard that the Antichrist is coming, even now many antichrists have come, by which we know that it is the last hour."*

(d) (Revelation 13:1-8) *"Then I [John] stood on the sand of the sea. And I saw a beast rising up out of the sea, having seven heads and ten horns, and on his horns ten crowns, and on his heads a blasphemous name. Now the beast which I saw was like a leopard, his feet were like the feet of a bear, and his mouth like the mouth of a lion. The dragon gave him his power, his throne, and great authority. And I saw one of his heads as if it had been mortally wounded, and his deadly wound was healed. And all the world marveled and followed the beast. So they worshiped the dragon who gave authority to the beast; and they worshiped the beast, saying, 'Who is like the beast? Who is able to make war with him?' And he was given a mouth speaking great things and blasphemies, and he was given authority to continue for forty-two months. Then he opened his mouth in blasphemy against God, to blaspheme His name, His tabernacle, and those who dwell in heaven. It was granted to him to make war with the saints and to overcome them. And authority was given him over every tribe, tongue, and nation. All who dwell on the earth will worship him, whose names have not been written in the Book of Life of the Lamb slain from the foundation of the world."*

(e) (Revelation 17:6-14) *"I [John] saw the woman, drunk with the blood of the saints and with the blood of the martyrs of Jesus. And when I saw her, I marveled with great amazement. But the angel said to me, 'Why did you marvel? I will tell you the mystery of the woman and of the beast that carries her, which has the seven heads and the ten horns. The beast that you saw was, and is not, and will ascend out of the bottomless pit and go to perdition. And those who dwell on the earth will marvel, whose names are not written in the Book of Life from the foundation of the world, when they see the beast that was, and is not, and yet is. Here is the mind which has wisdom: The seven heads are seven mountains on which the woman sits. There are also seven kings. Five have fallen, one is, and the other has not yet come. And when he comes, he must continue a short time. The beast that was, and is not, is himself also the eighth, and is of the seven, and is going to perdition. The ten horns which you saw are ten kings who have received no kingdom as yet, but they receive authority for one hour as kings with the beast. These are of one mind, and they will give their power and authority to the beast. These will make war with the Lamb, and the Lamb will overcome them, for He is Lord of lords and King of kings; and those who are with Him are called, chosen, and faithful.'"*

# LESSON 18

**PROPHETS OF ISRAEL**

7. Read Daniel 7:26,27. Again, of what does God want Daniel (and us) to be assured in the midst of these troubling prophecies of the future?

**THIRD DAY: Read Daniel 8**

8. Daniel received a vision detailing events, most of which would occur with amazing accuracy about four hundred years later. Some details seem to have a double application—to a then-future leader and to an end-time leader. Fill in the blanks.

_____(a) The city in which Daniel found himself in his vision was this.

_____(b) These details were given about the ram in the vision.

_____(c) These details were given about the male goat coming from the west.

_____(d) These details were given about the *"little horn"* in the vision.

_____(e) This was the number of days (literally *"evenings and mornings"*) that the *"little horn"* would stop the temple sacrifices and oppress the Jews.

_____(f) Gabriel told Daniel that the vision described would happen at this time.

_____(g) The ram with two horns symbolized this.

_____(h) The goat with one horn replaced by four represented this.

_____(i) This would happen in the latter time of the divided Greek kingdom.

_____(j) This was Daniel's reaction.

1. 2300
2. a coming ruler of Greece who would be replaced by four kings who would not have his original power
3. the kings of Media and Persia
4. He fainted and was sick for days, astonished by the vision.
5. Shushan, Persia
6. He had two horns, the higher coming up later, and pushed westward, northward, and southward and no one could stop him. He became great.
7. He emerged out of one of the goat's four horns and grew great toward the south, toward the east, and toward the Glorious Land (Israel). He exalted himself even against God and cast down the temple and stopped the sacrifices.
8. He had one notable horn and came without touching the ground to fight the ram. He broke both horns of the ram and none could stop him. He grew very great and then the large horn was broken and replaced by four other notable horns.
9. A king shall arise having fierce features who understands sinister schemes, has mighty power (not his own), and shall destroy, prosper, and thrive. He will use deceit and come against the Jews and the Lord Himself.
10. the time of the end

Page 86

# LESSON 18 — PROPHETS OF ISRAEL

## FOURTH DAY: Read Daniel 9

9. Read Daniel 9:1-23. What had Daniel been reading that caused him to begin this particular prayer for his nation?

10. After beginning with a statement of praise in verse 4, what did Daniel continue with in verses 5-15?

11. What did Daniel's use of *"us"* and *"our"* mean to you?

12. (a) What did Daniel request from God in verses 16-19?

    (b) On what grounds did he dare to ask God for this?

13. Read Daniel 9:20-23.
    (a) What words or phrases indicate how quickly God responded to Daniel's prayer?

    (b) What can you learn from this?

## FIFTH DAY: Finish Daniel 9

14. Read Daniel 9:24. The angel revealed to Daniel a time-frame in which some very specific things were to happen in Jerusalem, the *"holy city."* What things were determined?
    (a) to finish

    (b) to make

    (c) to make

Page 87

# LESSON 18
## PROPHETS OF ISRAEL

(d) to bring in

(e) to seal up

(f) and to anoint

15. In answer to Daniel's prayer for Israel, God revealed His plans for their future. Read Daniel 9:25-27. (**Note:** Seventy "weeks" in Hebrew is literally seventy "sevens." This is commonly accepted as referring to years, so seventy sevens or seventy "weeks of years" would be 490 years.) The prophecy lists certain events that will occur during three divisions of that time period of 490 years. Describe them.
    (a) The event that begins the first period of seven "sevens" or 49 years:

    (b) The event that occurs at the end of the next period of 62 "sevens" or 434 years:

    (c) The event that will occur in the last seven years or "week":

    (d) The event that will occur in the middle of that last seven years or "week":

16. That last "week" or last seven years of Daniel's prophecy was also described in the following passages of Scripture, confirming Daniel's vision. Match the following terms used to describe this terrible last "week" with the verse(s) from which they were taken.

    _____(a) the great tribulation
    _____(b) time of trouble
    _____(c) time of Jacob's trouble
    _____(d) world-wide hour of trouble

    1. (Jeremiah 30:7) *"Alas! For that day is great, so that none is like it; and it is the time of Jacob's trouble, but he shall be saved out of it"*

    2. (Daniel 12:1) *"At that time Michael shall stand up, the great prince who stands watch over the sons of your people; and there shall be a time of trouble, such as never was since there was a nation, even to that time. And at that time your people shall be delivered, every one who is found written in the book."*

# LESSON 18 — PROPHETS OF ISRAEL

    3. (Revelation 3:10) *"Because you have kept My command to persevere, I also will keep you from the hour of trial which shall come upon the whole world, to test those who dwell on the earth."*

    4. (Revelation 7:13,14) *"Then one of the elders answered, saying to me [John], 'Who are these arrayed in white robes, and where did they come from?' And I said to him, 'Sir, you know.' So he said to me, 'These are the ones who come out of the great tribulation, and washed their robes and made them white in the blood of the Lamb.'"*

17. These prophecies could have been used to calculate the exact date of Messiah's arrival in Jerusalem! God did not want them to miss their Messiah. However, Jesus wept when He entered the city centuries later because the nation had missed the day of His visitation (Luke 19:41-44). For a little challenge, do the math yourself to calculate the date of Christ's entry into Jerusalem prophesied in Daniel. If you can figure it out, shouldn't the Jewish leaders have been able to do so?

    (**Note:** Hebrew years are 360 days so some adjustment is necessary. Also one year must be added for the transition from B.C. to A.D.)

    (a) 49 + 434 = 483 Hebrew years x 360 days = _____ days.

    (b) _____ divided by 365 days = _____ years (in our time).
        [answer from (a)]

    (c) _____ years - 445 B.C.(when the streets and walls of Jerusalem had been
        [answer from (b)]    completed according to Daniel 9:25) = _____ + 1 =
    A.D. _____ the year Christ officially presented Himself to the leaders of Jerusalem.

18. If *"Messiah the Prince"* is Jesus, then who is the *"prince who is to come"* who makes a covenant for the last seven years of this prophecy but breaks it in the middle? (**Hint:** See Revelation 13:1-8.)

19. Use your column references or concordance to locate the New Testament reference to the *"abomination of desolation"* mentioned in Daniel 9:27 and write it out below.

20. Using just a few sentences, summarize what Daniel learned in answer to his prayers for Israel about their future.

# Notes

## DANIEL 7:15-9:27

### More about the Fourth Beast (Daniel 7:15-28)

Deeply troubled by the vision of the four beasts, especially by the last one, Daniel asked for help from *"one of those who stood by,"* presumably an angel. The interpretation came from him. First, the angel summarized the entire vision. All four beasts were kings who would rise out of the earth and rule for a time, but, in the end, the *"saints of the most High"* (his fellow Israelites) would not only receive the kingdom for themselves but also possess it eternally.

While this summary was helpful, Daniel wanted to know more of the details, especially about how to interpret the fourth beast who differed from all the others. Daniel suddenly recalled that in his vision, the other horn, the one that came later and uprooted three of the first ones, was greater than the others and made war against the saints, even prevailing against them until he was stopped by order of the *"Ancient of Days"* (Daniel 7:22).

The angel continued his explanation. The fourth beast was the fourth world-kingdom, and its ten horns represented the ten kings that would come out of it. Since ten kings would rise out of one kingdom, they must have something in common, if not just geographic location then perhaps the same political ideology. Another king would come to power after the ten, but he would be different from them and able to subdue three of them.

Besides political power, this *"little horn,"* who would grow big, had intelligence (*"eyes of a man"*), communication skills (*"speak pompous words against the Most High"*), and a desire to destroy the saints of God (Daniel 7:25). He will even attempt to change times and law, both of which had been established by Israel's God from civilization's earliest days. However, this last leader associated with the last beast would not have the last word. God would stop his attack on the saints (from Daniel's point of view this always meant the Jews), judge him, condemn him, and consign him to the *"burning flame"* (Daniel 7:11,21,22,27).

### Some More Information from History

Daniel's vision of the coming fourth beast seemed to encompass more than one phase of world rule. From history we know that Rome followed Greece into power and dramatically increased its world influence. After just a few centuries, the mighty Roman empire crumbled, but it left in its wake many nations which would remain interrelated because of their earlier union through Rome. The modern countries making up Europe as well as some in Northern Africa, Asia Minor, and Western Asia are the former people-groups that were once consolidated under Roman rule. Since January 1, 1999, many of them share a common currency called the euro and meet jointly to consider matters of mutual interest.

While the rise of Rome has already occurred in history to fulfill part of Daniel's vision, the prophecies about the ten kings and the terrible *"little horn"* have not been fulfilled as yet. So this seems to be another phase of Daniel's vision, perhaps not understood by even him at the time. Yet many other Scriptures indicate that such a man will come to power and cause great grief to Israel. Some of his titles are *"the Antichrist," "man of sin," "son of perdition," "mouth speaking pompous words," "little horn," "lawless one,"* and *"the beast"* (2 Thessalonians 2:3-8; 1 John 2:18; Revelation 13:1-8; Daniel 7:8). There was some comfort in the fact given by the angel that his influence or authority over God's people would be limited to *"time and times and half a time"* (interpreted as three-and-a-half years when compared to Daniel 9:27 [mid-week or half of seven years] or Revelation 12:6 [Jewish months are 30 days]). At the end of that time, the *"little horn"* will be silenced forever as the saints of God are saved and given an everlasting kingdom from God Himself. Having received the whole interpretation, Daniel was still greatly troubled but kept the matter in his heart (Daniel 7:28).

### Skeptics Hate It (Daniel 8)

The very specific fulfillment, verifiable from history, of Daniel's prophecies from chapter eight infuriate those who want to deny the accuracy of Scripture. Skeptics declare it impossible that Daniel could have written this in the sixth century B.C.; they claim it had to have been written after-the-fact, some time after Medo-Persia and Greece came to power in the third and fourth centuries B.C. However, many Bibles students accept the fact that God not only knows what is going to happen before it does but also has had it recorded by His prophets, primarily to bolster the faith of His people so that they can trust Him even more.

## The Vision (Daniel 8:1-14)

This vision was given to Daniel in the third year of Belshazzar's reign. In it, Daniel was transported to a city in Persia called Shushan. There, beside the River Ulai, he saw a ram with unequal horns, the higher of the pair emerging last. Pushing west, north, and south, the ram was able to conquer everything in his way; he became great (Daniel 8:3,4). Next, Daniel saw a male goat approaching from the west, crossing the whole earth without even touching the ground. That goat had a *"notable horn between his eyes."* The goat furiously attacked the ram, breaking its two horns, and completely conquering it.

Afterward, the male goat grew even greater, but his large horn was broken and four more *"notable"* horns came up in its place, toward the four winds of heaven. Out of one of the four horns came a little one which grew very great toward the south, east, and toward the Glorious Land of Israel. It was able to reach even to heaven and cast down some of the host and stars, which it soon trampled. In verse eleven, the "it" became "he" and this person was described as even opposing the *"Prince of the host."* He also removed the daily sacrifices at the temple and destroyed the holy sanctuary. This person had an army at his disposal, but his power over the people and the sanctuary was to be limited to two thousand and three hundred days (literally, evenings and mornings).

## The Interpretation (Daniel 8:15-22)

No less a personage than the arch-angel Gabriel was sent to Daniel to interpret the vision. First, he made clear to Daniel about the time-frame: *"the vision refers to the time of the end"* or, in verse 19, the prophetic timing described as the *"latter time of the indignation."* Simply put, the two horns of the ram represented the kings of Media and Persia. The male goat was the kingdom of Greece, with the large horn representing its first great king, known from history to have been Alexander the Great. After his death, four kingdoms would be formed from his, as four of his generals divided and took over his realm. Their names were Ptolemy, Seleucus, Lysimachus, and Cassander, but their collective power never matched that held by Alexander (Daniel 8:22).

The fulfillment of the first part of the vision was fairly easy to trace, but Daniel was given additional information about a *"horn"* or king who would arise out of one of the four divisions of the old Greek empire (Daniel 7:8). His influence or dominion would grow southward, eastward, and then finally toward Israel. A limit was put on his dominion. The modern translations read 2,300 days or less than six and a half years, but the literal Hebrew reads 2,300 evenings and mornings which might cut the time in half, to less than three and a half years. Anyway, this person, who would dare to claim equality with God (Daniel 8:11), would stop the daily sacrifices in the rebuilt temple in Jerusalem. Not only that, but he would also *"cast down"* God's sanctuary there, attempt to destroy truth, and trample God's host.

Historically, this seems to all have come true under the wicked rulership of the eighth ruler of the Seleucid dynasty whose name was Antiochus IV, also called Epiphanes.

He was not a legal heir to the throne, but used under-handed tactics to rise to power. Once ruling, he attacked Egypt on the south, Armenia and Eymais on the east, and then tried to brutally enforce his own religious policies on the Jews regathered in Israel. (Note: For very interesting reading on this time-period, read 1 Maccabees 1:29-64 which can be found among the books of the **Apocrypha**. They are not accepted as part of our Bible but still provide some helpful background information on this time-period.) Antiochus had a pig offered on God's holy altar which was an unspeakable **abomination** in the sight of the Jews. He also launched a terrible persecution of the Jews that lasted from 171 to 165 B.C. He died suddenly of either a fall or some sort of terrible disease, accounts differ, but he was not killed by his enemies which was in keeping with the prophecy: *"he shall be broken without human means"* (Daniel 8:25). The Jews then undertook to repair and cleanse the temple and in so doing, experienced a miracle as the insufficient supply of sacred lamp oil lasted the eight days necessary to formulate more. This event is celebrated by Jews today as the Feast of Dedication or Hanukkah.

## Antiochus and Antichrist (Daniel 8:23-27)

The prophetic description of the fierce leader with *"sinister schemes"* of this passage was initially fulfilled in the actions of Antiochus Epiphanes about 380 years after Daniel recorded it. However, many see in its frightening details a further prophecy descriptive of the actions of the Antichrist of the very last days. He, like Antiochus, will be allowed to severely persecute the Jews, but only for three and a half years. The Antichrist would also *"understand sinister schemes,"* have mighty power (the source of which was not his own), destroy the mighty along with the holy people, use cunning, *"cause deceit to prosper under his rule,"* exalt himself, challenge the *"Prince of princes,"* and finally be destroyed *"without human means."* These have been terrifying details, indeed, about that future leader, but God emphasized more than once that this evil leader would be finally and utterly destroyed. God is sovereign over all, and we can trust Him with the future.

## Daniel's Discovery (Daniel 9:1,2)

It was about 538 B.C. when Daniel recorded this chapter; Daniel had been a captive in Babylon since 605 B.C. As he read the prophecies of Jeremiah, he realized that the seventy years were almost over and that the promised deliverance had to be near. However, from the information he had received from the previously recorded visions, he knew that some terrible times still awaited his nation. So, confused but wanting God to end the exile, he approached God in prayer. The following excerpts from Jeremiah were probably among the passages that motivated Daniel to find out more.

*"And this whole land shall be a **desolation** and an astonishment, and these nations shall serve the king of Babylon seventy years"* (Jeremiah 25:11).

*"Thus says the LORD of hosts, the God of Israel, to all who were carried away captive, whom I have caused to be carried away from Jerusalem to Babylon: Build houses and dwell in them; plant gardens and eat their fruit. Take wives and beget sons and daughters; and take wives for your sons and give your daughters to husbands, so that they may bear sons and daughters—that you may be increased there, and not diminished. And seek the peace of the city where I have caused you to be carried away captive, and pray to the LORD for it; for in its peace you will have peace. For thus says the LORD of hosts, the God of Israel: Do not let your prophets and your diviners who are in your midst deceive you, nor listen to your dreams which you cause to be dreamed. For they prophesy falsely to you in My name; I have not sent them, says the LORD. For thus says the LORD: After seventy years are completed at Babylon, I will visit you and perform My good word toward you, and cause you to return to this place"* (Jeremiah 29:4-10).

## Daniel's Prayer (Daniel 9:3-19)

Praise always brings the proper perspective to our problems, and Daniel used it at the beginning of his prayer to focus his thoughts on the greatness of his covenant God, who always shows mercy to those who love Him and keep His commandments. Next, he began a long corporate confession of Israel's national sins, using "us" and "our" to include himself among the sinners. He verbally acknowledged the fact that God's judgment on Jerusalem had been righteous because they had broken covenant with Him. Daniel noted that God had only brought on them what He had warned in Scripture that He would. Even after the fall of Jerusalem, Daniel confessed, the nation had not turned back in repentance to God to receive forgiveness for their sins and understanding of all that had happened (Daniel 9:13). Boldly moving forward to his actual petition, Daniel asked God to turn His fury away from Jerusalem and shine His face again on His sanctuary there. Not for the sake of His wicked people, Daniel could not ask that, but for the sake of His own good name, His own reputation among the people of the world. It was grievous to Daniel that the city that bore the name of the Most High God lay in ruins with its people scattered.

## God's Answer (Daniel 9:20-24)

God was evidently pleased with Daniel's prayer because, while Daniel was still praying, God dispatched the angel Gabriel to give him understanding about the future trouble and final deliverance He had planned for Israel.

Just as Israel had been exiled in Babylon for their failure to observe seventy sabbatical years, which would have covered a 490-year period (See Leviticus 25:2-7.), so God had set aside a 490-year period or 70 "weeks" of years in which to complete His plans for Israel, *"to finish the transgression, to make an end of sins, to make reconciliation for iniquity, to bring in everlasting righteousness, to seal up vision and prophecy, and to anoint the Most Holy,"* and give them their eternal kingdom. The 490 years were not to run consecutively but to be divided into three periods.

## Phase One (Daniel 9:25)

The prophetic stopwatch would start ticking when a command was given to restore and rebuild Jerusalem, including her street and wall (literally, open square and moat). There were at least four different commands issued concerning the rebuilding of the wall of Jerusalem, first by Cyrus, then Darius, and finally Artaxerxes, all rulers of Medo-Persia. However, only one of these included the rebuilding of the wall of Jerusalem which was necessary before a moat or open square could be defined and constructed. This command was issued by King Artaxerxes in 445 B.C. The prophecy stated that from the time that that command was issued until Messiah would be revealed to Israel was a period of seven "sevens" or forty-nine years and then sixty-two "sevens" or 434 years. Bible historians believe that the first forty-nine years covered the repair and reconstruction of Jerusalem which ended with a covenant renewal celebration in Jerusalem in 396 B.C. The 434 years would follow that.

## Phase Two (Daniel 9:26)

It should be noted that a Hebrew year was 360 days long, and a Hebrew month was thirty days long. Following the forty-nine years for the rebuilding of Jerusalem, including wall and street, was to be a period of sixty-two more "weeks" or 434 more years before the Messiah appeared (Daniel 9:25). In the late 1800's, a Bible scholar named Sir Robert Anderson calculated with these figures that the coming of the Messiah would be in A.D. 32, even noting the date as April the sixth. Some scholars differ a year or two from this figure, but even the "untrained" mathematician can calculate the time of the death of Messiah fairly accurately with Daniel's information. Astronomical data limits the number of choices for the date to be between A.D. 26 and A.D. 30. Regardless of the year in our calendar, however, Jesus fulfilled Zechariah 9:9 on the exact day that God had ordained. He entered Jerusalem on a donkey to be identified publicly as Israel's long-awaited King Messiah. A few days later, His crucifixion on Passover fulfilled Daniel 9:26: *"And after the sixty-two weeks Messiah shall be cut off, but not for Himself...."*

The prophecy stated that the death of Messiah would be followed by the destruction of Jerusalem and the temple by the *"people of the prince who is to come."* From history, we know that the Romans destroyed Jerusalem and the temple in A.D. 70, so a clue is given here that the *"prince who is to come"* would be associated with that Roman empire.

## Phase Three (Daniel 9:27)

The last "week" or seven years that remained of the 490 God had appointed to finish all the prophecies and bring about the fulfillment of all promises to Israel, appears to be yet in the future. The cosmic stopwatch seemed to stop for Israel at the Cross, since they did not accept their Messiah. This gap that has occurred since the fulfillment of the first two phases can be termed the Church Age or Age of Grace. Daniel did not know about this, nor did anyone else in the Old Testament. Paul, in the New Testament, explained that it had been a mystery, known only to God (Ephesians 3:1-13). During this time God's program for reaching the Gentiles with the gospel is in progress. Israel disappeared as a nation for nineteen centuries as the Gentile nations rose and fell without even having to consider her. Only in 1948 did she re-emerge as a recognizable national entity. Yet, the final seven years of Israel's—as well as the world's—existence on the present earth were outlined briefly in Daniel 9:27. A world-leader out of the old Roman empire will rise; he is called here *"the prince who is to come."* He will make a covenant or treaty with Israel for a seven-year period, but he will break it at the mid-point, after three and a half years, by stopping the sacrifices and offerings in the rebuilt temple in Jerusalem and committing the worst abomination there in history. This will bring about its complete desolation in the eyes of God's people. The word *"wing"* in the passage is a superlative meaning, in this particular context, the worst possible abomination.

## What's Next?

All but the last seven years of the 490 Daniel was told about have come to pass exactly as prophesied. We can be assured that the final seven will be fulfilled just as perfectly. In the meantime, in this Age of Grace for which no definite length of time has been set in prophecy, we are to be busy about our Father's business. Our security as we face the final years of earth or the final years of our own lives is to be in the Ancient of Days who sovereignly rules for His glory and for His children's good.

---

### VOCABULARY

1. **abomination:** anything that excites disgust, hatred, or loathing
2. **Apocrypha:** those books of the Septuagint included in the Vulgate but rejected by Protestants as uncanonical because they are not in the Hebrew Scriptures
3. **desolation:** the condition of being ruined or deserted

# Notes

# Notes

# PROPHETS OF ISRAEL — LESSON 19

## Daily Bible Study Questions

**Study Procedure:** Read the Scripture references before answering questions. Unless otherwise instructed, use the Bible only in answering questions. Some questions may be more difficult than others but try to answer as many as you can. Pray for God's wisdom and understanding as you study and don't be discouraged if some answers are not obvious at first.

### THIS WEEK'S MEMORY VERSE:

(Daniel 12:1) *"At that time Michael shall stand up, the great prince who stands watch over the sons of your people; and there shall be a time of trouble, such as never was since there was a nation, even to that time. And at that time your people shall be delivered, every one who is found written in the book."*

### FIRST DAY: Review of Daniel 7:15-9:27

1. Matching:

    _____(a) Ancient of Days (Chapter 7)

    _____(b) Son of Man (Chapter 7)

    _____(c) little horn of the fourth beast (Chapter 7); the prince who is to come (Chapter 9)

    _____(d) the saints (Chapters 7 and 8)

    _____(e) the ram with two horns (Chapter 8)

    _____(f) the goat with one, then four horns (Chapter 8)

    _____(g) the notable horn which came out of one of the four horns of the goat (Chapter 8)

    _____(h) the angel who helped Daniel understand (Chapters 8 and 9)

    _____(i) the prophet whose work Daniel was reading which caused him to pray (Chapter 9)

    1. Godly Jews
    2. God the Father
    3. Alexander the Great, king of Greece
    4. Jesus
    5. Gabriel
    6. Jeremiah
    7. King of Medo-Persia
    8. Antichrist
    9. Antiochus Epiphanes

2. Pick at least one personality from last week's lesson and write several facts which you learned about him. Give some Scripture references where that person was mentioned.

Page 97

# LESSON 19 — PROPHETS OF ISRAEL

**SECOND DAY: Read Daniel 10 and begin Daniel 11**

3. Read Daniel 10:1-9. In this chapter, the Holy Spirit has pulled back the curtain to reveal the spiritual warfare that had been occurring during this time in the heavenly realm.

   (**Note:** It was 536 B.C., two years after some of the exiles had been allowed to return to Jerusalem under the leadership of Zerubbabel to start rebuilding the temple.)

   (a) What had Daniel been doing before he saw the glorious spiritual figure?

   (b) What was Daniel's response to seeing this marvelous personage?

4. Read Daniel 10:10-13.
   (a) What did the heavenly messenger call Daniel?

   (b) How long had the heavenly messenger been trying to get to Daniel?

   (c) What had hindered him and how did he get away? [**Note:** Michael is a high-order of angel assigned to the defense of Israel. (See Daniel 10:21, Daniel 12:1, Jude 1:9, and Revelation 12:7.) The kings of Persia (Daniel 10:13) and princes of Persia and Greece (Daniel 10:20) refer to the demonic spirits assigned to those places.]

5. Read Daniel 10:14-21.
   (a) What had this angel been sent to tell Daniel?

   (b) What kind actions were shown to Daniel in his shocked and weakened state by *"one having the likeness of the sons of men"*? Give verses.

# LESSON 19
**PROPHETS OF ISRAEL**

6. What interesting information about the spiritual realm is revealed in Daniel 10:20,21 and Daniel 11:1?

7. Read Daniel 11:2-28. Read through this very detailed prophecy of a then still future period of history. Bible skeptics hate this passage because every detail can be proved to have been fulfilled by consulting available historical records, even though it was written in 536 B.C., long before any of it occurred. Give the verses where the following are mentioned.
    (a) the fourth ruler of Persia (Xerxes)

    (b) a mighty king whose kingdom was divided four ways, but not among his own descendants (This was Alexander the Great.)

    (c) the king of the North (Syria)

    (d) the king of the South (Egypt)

    (e) the *"vile person"* that comes to power (Antiochus Epiphanes)

    (f) the prince of the covenant (Israel's high priest)

**THIRD DAY: Continue in Daniel 11**
8. Read Daniel 11:29-35. This section of prophecy was fulfilled when Antiochus Epiphanes (175-164 B.C.) cruelly attacked Israel.
    (a) List some of the specific things he did to the temple.

    (b) List some of the things he did to God's people.

9. Read Daniel 11:36-39. List several facts about or characteristics of the king described here.

10. Who, from earlier lessons on Daniel's prophecies, does this man resemble? (See Daniel 7:8,24,25.)

Page 99

# LESSON 19       PROPHETS OF ISRAEL

11. Read Daniel 11:40,41. When, *"at the time of the end,"* the king of the South (Egypt) and the king of the North (Syria) come like a whirlwind to attack the evil king, who wins?

12. Read Daniel 11:41-43. The other nations mentioned as taking part in these end-time events are listed below. Write a short explanation beside each as to what happens to them.
    (a) Edom, Moab, Ammon

    (b) Egypt

    (c) Libya and Ethiopia

13. Read Daniel 11:44,45.
    (a) What will divert the attention of the evil king?

    (b) What will finally happen to him?

**FOURTH DAY: Read Daniel 12**

14. Read Daniel 12:1. *"At that time"* makes this verse apply to the *"time of the end"* introduced in Daniel 11:40. List the things that will occur then.

15. Read Daniel 12:2,3. What is described here?

16. Read Daniel 12:4-12. Daniel was told to seal up the book of prophecies he had written until the time of the end. But an angel asked another question.
    (a) What was it?

    (b) How was it answered?

Page 100

# LESSON 19 — PROPHETS OF ISRAEL

17. Daniel still did not understand (which is a bit of a comfort to us all!) and asked *"My lord, what shall be the end of these things?"* (verse 8).
    (a) What was he told to do personally?

    (b) What final details was he given to record?

    (c) What personal promise was he given?

18. Sum up your thoughts about the book of Daniel. What did you learn? Why do you think it is still important to study?

## FIFTH DAY: Read Haggai 1 and 2

19. Read Haggai 1:1-15.
    (a) What problem did the Lord have the prophet Haggai address that concerned the Jews who had returned to Jerusalem to rebuild the temple?

    (b) How did the people respond to Haggai's message?

    (c) How did God help them?

20. Read Haggai 2:1-9. After they resumed work on the temple, God had Haggai give another message to them.
    (a) What was discouraging them?

    (b) What did God tell them to encourage them?

# LESSON 19  PROPHETS OF ISRAEL

21. Read Haggai 2:10-14. In the third month of their work, God had Haggai conduct a hypothetical question-answer interview with the priests.
    (a) What point was God making about the spiritual condition of the people there?

    (b) Although they had been obeying God outwardly in rebuilding the temple, what more did He want from them?

    (c) What could their spiritual "uncleanness" do to their work?

22. Read Haggai 2:15-23.
    (a) What did God promise to start doing for His people immediately?

    (b) What promises did He make about their future?

23. Read Matthew 1:12,13 and Luke 3:27 and find out how God kept His word to bless Zerubbabel, who was governor at this time and led the people in obeying the Lord. Write what you find out below.

24. At the time of Haggai, God's people were at first distracted from their main task, then discouraged, and then spiritually defiled. What did you learn from the book of Haggai that would help you when you find yourself in a similar frame-of-mind?
    (a) distracted

    (b) discouraged

    (c) defiled

Page 102

# Notes

## DANIEL 10-12 AND HAGGAI 1-2

### Still Being Used by God (Daniel 10:1-11)

The date for chapter ten was given as the third year of Cyrus' reign in Persia. This was 536 B.C., just two years after the Jews had been allowed to return to Jerusalem to rebuild the temple. (See 2 Chronicles 36:22,23.) After immediately building an altar, beginning sacrifices, and laying the foundation, the people quickly got distracted and discouraged, and, as the study of Haggai revealed, began only to construct houses for themselves. Word of this may have increased Daniel's grief at a time when he was already troubled by the visions of Israel's distant future he had just received. He did what we have come to expect from him since studying his writings; he went to the Lord in prayer about it all, showing the intensity of his concern by fasting for three weeks.

At the end of the three weeks, when he was outside by the River Tigris, he had an incredible vision of a supernatural personage. The figure was clothed in linen and girded in gold, with a body like **beryl**, face like lightning, eyes like fire, arms and feet like polished brass, and a voice powerfully magnificent. Only Daniel saw this man; his companions just sensed the presence and fled in fear. Daniel almost lost consciousness, collapsing to the ground in wonder, but a hand touched him and a voice called him *"greatly beloved"* (verse 11).

### Spiritual Warfare (Daniel 10:12-11:1)

Daniel's prayer not only provided him with additional insight into future events but also allowed an opportunity for the Holy Spirit to reveal some of the mysterious activities in the realm of the supernatural for those who would study this account. The glorious personage told Daniel that he had set out to answer Daniel three weeks earlier, *"from the first day that you set your heart to understand, and to humble yourself before your God"* (verse 12). (Note: Some see here a pre-incarnate appearance of Jesus Himself, while others think Daniel was visited by a very high-ranking angel. This is because the heavenly being had been detained and needed help getting the victory. Those holding this view believe Jesus would have needed no such help.) The delay had been caused by spiritual warfare with demonic powers in charge of Persia. Satan had not wanted Daniel to receive anymore information about future events, especially detailing his evil actions against Israel, and had sent forces to stop the heavenly messenger. Interestingly, this passage revealed that there are most likely spiritual battles going on around us all the time, of which we are unaware.

The heavenly being also revealed that, in the year Darius the Mede conquered Babylon (Daniel 10:21 and 11:1), he and Michael had to fight spiritual forces opposing that change in power. God had prophesied it, but Satan tried to stop it, no doubt because the new Persian leadership would allow the Jews to go back and rebuild the temple and resume their right worship of God.

The glorious personage told Daniel he had come to make him *"understand what will happen to your people in the latter days, for the vision refers to many days yet to come"* (verse 14). Daniel admitted that it was because of the vision of such things that he had been overcome with sorrow and weakness. The heavenly emissary had to touch and then speak to Daniel to strengthen him enough to listen. He told Daniel that he had to leave soon to face another battle with the demonic princes of Persia and Greece.

The mention of Michael as *"your prince"* (verse 21) in the messenger's conversation with Daniel confirmed another verse found in Daniel 12:1 which described Michael as *"the great prince who stands watch over the sons of your people."* Jude 1:9 identified Michael as an **archangel**, powerful enough to be dispatched against Satan himself. Revelation 12:7 described him as having other angels under his authority who help him engage in spiritual battle. All of these details open our eyes a bit to a sometimes forgotten reality about which many Scriptures have been given to make us aware. Ponder this one from the New Testament, from Ephesians 6:12,13:

> *For we do not wrestle against flesh and blood, but against **principalities**, against powers, against the rulers of the darkness*

*of this age, against spiritual hosts of wickedness in the heavenly places. Therefore take up the whole armor of God, that you may be able to withstand in the evil day, and having done all, to stand.*

## Pre-Written History (Daniel 11:2-45)

This vision was so specific in its details about the struggles between Persia and Greece for dominance and the **intrigue** involved among the future rulers of Greece that John Calvin spent forty pages detailing the fulfillment! Here, just a synopsis will be given of the major events prophesied and fulfilled.

**Kings of Persia (Daniel 11:2):** The three Persian kings who would follow Cyrus, the king in Daniel's day, were Cambyses (529-523 B.C.), Gaumata, an impostor (523-522 B.C.), and Darius the Great, who assassinated Gaumata and took the throne (522-485 B.C.). The fourth, *"richer than them all,"* who stirred *"up all against the realm of Greece,"* was Xerxes (485-464 B.C.). He prepared a huge army to invade Greece in 480 B.C. but was tragically unsuccessful. Xerxes' failure left Persia open to the attacks by Greece a century later.

**Alexander the Great (Daniel 11:3,4):** These verses referred to Alexander the Great who ultimately conquered Persia and other lands, beginning his campaigns in 334 B.C. However, he died at just 32 years of age in 323 B.C. All his relatives were murdered, leaving his kingdom to be divided among four of his generals: Antipater, Lysimachus, Ptolemy, and Seleucus.

**Alexander's Divided Empire (Daniel 11:5-20):** These verses detailed the struggles between the two strongest of the four divisions of Alexander's Greek empire. Ptolemy's division, headquartered in Egypt, and the leader, here called the king of the South, fought continually with the division held by Seleucus, which included Syria, the leader of which was called the king of the North. The conflicts between these two would have the most direct effects on Israel, which is probably why they were included in these prophecies to Daniel. These verses foretell in detail about the intrigue of that time: marriage alliances, murders, and other assorted political maneuverings.

Verse fourteen noted that some Jews would try to intervene during that time but would fail. This happened during the time of Antiochus the Great. Some Jewish rebels fought with him to take Israel away from Egyptian control. They mistakenly thought an alliance with Syria would be more beneficial, but it just resulted in their being put under the evil authority of Antiochus Epiphanes some years later. Another example of the precision of this prophecy can be seen in the fulfillment of verse 20, which prophesied a king coming into office who would impose taxes on Israel (*"the glorious kingdom"*) but would himself be soon destroyed, but not in battle. Renald Showers, of Friends of Israel Gospel Ministry, in his book on Daniel, *The Most High God*, gave these details on page 156:

> Antiochus the Great was succeeded by his son, Seleucus IV Philopater (197-176 B.C.). The Romans required him to pay a 1,000-talent tribute each year. This forced him to levy heavy taxes on the peoples of his kingdom. Seleucus sent his prime minister, Heliodorus, to Jerusalem to take the wealth of the Temple treasury. A short time after this, Seleucus suddenly and mysteriously died, possibly of poisoning, in 176 B.C.

**Antiochus Epiphanes (Daniel 11:21-35):** Antiochus IV Epiphanes (175-164 B.C.) succeeded Seleucus IV Philopater as king of Syria. He was so evil that he was called "Epimanes," which meant "madman," by his contemporaries. Even though he was not the legal heir to the throne, he gained the position by flattery and court intrigue (verse 21). Intermittently, between his power struggles with his sometime-ally Egypt, Antiochus greatly oppressed Israel. He removed the high priest (*"the prince of the covenant"*) not once but twice, forbade proper worship, circumcision, and even the very existence of the Old Testament scrolls. He punished anyone who violated his bans with cruel tortures and death. Not only did he desecrate the temple by having a pig offered on the altar, but he also had an altar to Zeus erected over the burnt altar. This was the abomination of desolation mentioned in verse 31.

A Jewish priest named Mattathias Maccabeus and his five sons refused to forsake God's covenant.

Mattathias killed one of Antiochus' officers who tried to force him to offer pagan sacrifices, and he and his sons left their possessions and escaped to the mountains where they organized opposition to the blasphemous activities. Many of their group died for their faithful resistance, but not before many others were awakened to the seriousness of the controversy (verses 32-35).

**The Antichrist (Daniel 11:36-39):** While these verses continued to prophesy about the great wickedness of Antiochus Epiphanes, many also see in them a foreshadowing of some of the activities of the *"little horn"* or Antichrist who is to appear in the last days. These are some of the characteristics used in his description that seem prophetic of the coming *"little horn"* speaking blasphemies introduced earlier in Daniel 7:

1. Self-willed: This king will not serve under another for very long. He will insist on his own way (verse 36).

2. Ambitious, prideful: Humility will be absent from this ruler's nature as he insists on his own superiority to any other god and even over Israel's *"God of gods,"* against whom he will speak blasphemies (verse 36).

3. Self-sufficient: He will show no regard for the *"God of his fathers nor for the desire of women"* (verse 37).

4. Power-hungry: The only god he will recognize or honor is the god of power. With much wealth he will pursue it (verse 38).

5. Fearless: Without hesitation, he will attack *"the strongest fortresses with a foreign god"* causing changes in leadership and division of the land (verse 39).

**The Wicked King's Battle Plan (Daniel 11:40-45):** Many see this as unfulfilled prophecy and see the "him" as referring to the Antichrist of verses 36-39. If this is correct, and since a clear historical fulfillment does not exist for it as it does for all the prophecies prior to verse 36, then these verses do seem to outline a series of battles yet to be *"at the time of the end"* (verse 40). It is assumed that the symbolic language is to be translated as at the beginning of this chapter. If so, here is the summary: Egypt and Syria will come against the Antichrist with great resources, but he will still overwhelm them. He will enter Israel but without conquering Edom, Moab, or Ammon. He will turn and conquer the land of Egypt and remove all the things of value there. He will turn away from that area, leaving Libya and Ethiopia to follow him. News from the east and north will trouble him, and he will turn to face them, headquartering between Israel (perhaps because of the seven-year peace covenant he will have made with her—see Daniel 9:27) and the Mediterranean Sea. There he will come to his end with no one to save him.

## Hard Times Ahead (Daniel 12:1-12)

With all this end-time warfare prophesied in and around Israel, Daniel received word that Michael, God's archangel who stands watch over Israel, will himself arise to fight for God's people at that time. The fact that this spiritual battling will be necessary emphasized how serious the earthly battles for Israel will be. Daniel was told that there will be trouble *"such as never was since there was a nation"* (Daniel 12:1). However, ultimately, God's people will be delivered and everlasting life—for some in heaven and for some in hell—will commence (Daniel 12:2).

Daniel, still greatly troubled over all the details he had been shown, was told to seal up his book till a time when *"many shall run to and fro, and knowledge shall increase"* (Daniel 12:4). Two angels appeared and one asked the other, *"How long shall the fulfillment of these wonders be?"* In other words, how long would the terrible suffering of Israel last? The answer was that it would be for time, times, and half a time which would be the time when the holy people would have been completely shattered (Daniel 12:7).

Most often this is thought to indicate a period of three and a half years. This would correspond to the reference to the week (seven years) and middle of the week (three and a half years) mentioned about the same future events in Daniel 9:27. Through the trouble of that last terrible period, the righteous will be purified and the wicked will get more wicked. Wise people will be able to understand what is going on.

Another piece of the puzzle, still not explainable, was offered by the angel for Daniel to record. From the time that the daily sacrifices are stopped in the temple in Jerusalem because of the setting up of the abomination of desolation in the middle of the last seven years (Daniel 9:27), there will be three years and seven months (1,290 days) till the horror is all over. An unexplained blessing is further promised to those who endure two and a half months beyond that.

## Retirement at Last (Daniel 12:13)

After sixty years of faithfully serving God as His prophet, Daniel was finally told he could put down his pen and rest. He was promised that he would rise again *"at the end of the days"* to receive his eternal inheritance. How well Daniel rested with all these troubling visions about the terrible suffering yet in store for his people flowing through his head is questionable. However, as we should have learned from our study of his writings, God can be trusted to run the universe and bring His perfect will to pass. Ours is to be, like Daniel, fully available for the daily duties He assigns us, to know His Word and interpret it correctly for others, and to pray to Him for the understanding we need in facing troublesome times. God is on His throne, yet His people must often suffer. However, when the books are open, *"those who are wise shall shine like the brightness of the firmament, and those who turn many to righteousness"* (like Daniel!) *"like the stars forever and ever"* (Daniel 12:3).

## Hearing from Haggai

In contrast to the prophecies of Daniel, which spanned sixty years and applied to events still in the future, Haggai's prophecies spanned about four months and applied mainly to the people receiving them. Haggai was given his first message for the people in Jerusalem on August 8, 520 B.C., in the second year of King Darius' reign. This was eighteen years after the exiles had first been allowed to return to rebuild the temple. Initially, they had started. They built an altar, began the regular sacrifices, and even laid the foundation work, but the work was stopped by their enemies. (See Ezra 4:1-24.) It was this problem that Haggai was called to address.

## Distracted (Haggai 1:1-11)

If the New Testament had been available to Haggai, he could have used Matthew 6:33 for the text of this first message: *"But seek first the kingdom of God and His righteousness, and all these things shall be added to you."* The people of Jerusalem had become distracted from their primary priority—the rebuilding of God's temple. After being discouraged by the **slander** of their enemies which caused Artaxerxes, the reigning king in charge of the region, to sign an order to stop their work, they lost their focus and turned their attention to building homes for themselves. They excused any nudges from the Holy Spirit by saying, *"The time has not come, the time that the Lord's house should be built"* (Haggai 1:2).

Haggai pointed out that this focus on themselves, to the neglect of the Lord's house, was not paying off. They only had to open their eyes to see that they were not being blessed by God in their farm work, domestic duties, or wage earning (Haggai 1:6). He told them to consider their ways. God wanted them to get to work on His temple. He had been purposely withholding the rain and stopping the productivity of land and the thriving of animals to get their attention. They were to put His will first.

## Obedient (Haggai 1:12-15)

The governor of Judah, Zerubbabel, and the high priest Joshua, and all the remnant in Jerusalem obeyed God's message through Haggai. When this was evident, God had Haggai encourage them with this message: *"I am with you, says the LORD."* How quickly forgiveness is granted when God's people repent and obey! The Lord encouraged all of them, stirring their spirits, so that they came eagerly to work on His house.

## Discouraged (Haggai 2:1-9)

A little over a month later, when the work was well underway, Haggai was sent by the Lord to give the people another message. It appeared that the older workers, who had seen the glory of Solomon's temple years before, were disappointed and discouraged at the way the new one was shaping up. God told Haggai to encourage them: *"'Be strong, Zerubbabel...be strong, Joshua...be strong, all you people of the land...and work; for I am with you,' says the LORD of hosts."* He reminded them that He still owned all the gold and silver in the world (which He could make available if He wanted) and that He would again fill the place with His own glory. He assured them all that one day—it was still a little while off—*"the glory of this latter temple shall be greater than the former"* (Haggai 2:6,9), and not only His people in Israel but also people everywhere would come to His temple (Haggai 2:7). What a pep talk!

## Defiled (Haggai 2:10-14)

Two months later, Haggai was given another message for the people, but this was presented in a question-answer style to the priests. He posed **hypothetical** questions to them, which in modern-day terms could sound like these: "Does carrying something holy make the person carrying it holy?" The answer was no. He went further: "If holiness cannot be transferred from an object to a person, can uncleanness be transferred?" The answer was yes. Haggai acknowledged that that was correct and then made the application to the people building the temple. The handling of the holy stones did not make those handling them holy. However, the unholiness of the people did contaminate the holy work of temple-building. The solution? God wanted His people to seek spiritual holiness for themselves. He not only wanted their outward obedience, which they were now giving, but He also wanted their spiritual obedience.

This is still a very applicable illustration for our lives today. Doing God's work is not enough. Without the right spirit, we can actually contaminate the work. God wants personal holiness in His people before they put their hands to His tasks.

## Delighted (Haggai 2:15-19)

Now that the people were working spiritually and physically as God wished, He promised to pour His blessings on them. No longer would they find their bins half full and their vats half empty; abundance would return. So the New Testament words rang true even then: *"Seek first the kingdom of God and His righteousness"* and He will add all the rest!

## Delivered (Haggai 2:20-23)

Later that same day, Haggai received and delivered his last message to the people in Jerusalem. God had plans to shake the heavens and the earth until all the Gentile kingdoms were overthrown, allowing Israel to rise and rule. In that day, the Lord promised, He would bless Zerubbabel for his leadership, showing him off to the world like a signet ring. When both New Testament genealogies of Jesus are checked (Matthew 1:12,13 and Luke 3:27), one can find the name of Zerubbabel shining among the others, blessed by God as a part of the very lineage of Messiah, *"the Desire of All Nations,"* to whom the whole world will someday bow down.

Haggai's message was timely for his people but timeless for all who still read it. His words call us to seek God for help in dealing with all our distractions, discouragements, and defilements. We need only to repent and obey to experience the delight of God's favor and His deliverance from all that holds us back from His best.

---

### VOCABULARY

1. **archangel:** a very high-ranking angel; only mentioned in 1 Thessalonians 4:16 and Jude 1:9
2. **beryl:** a green, light blue, yellow, pink, or white silicate of aluminum and beryllium crystallizing in the hexagonal system; The aquamarine and emerald are varieties of it used for gems.
3. **hypothetical:** theoretical, based on a hypothesis
4. **intrigue:** the use of secret or underhanded means; plotting
5. **principalities:** the territories ruled over by princes
6. **slander:** an oral statement of a false, malicious, or defamatory nature, tending to damage another's reputation, means of livelihood, etc.

# Notes

# PROPHETS OF ISRAEL — LESSON 20

## Daily Bible Study Questions

**Study Procedure:** Read the Scripture references before answering questions. Unless otherwise instructed, use the Bible only in answering questions. Some questions may be more difficult than others but try to answer as many as you can. Pray for God's wisdom and understanding as you study and don't be discouraged if some answers are not obvious at first.

### THIS WEEK'S MEMORY VERSES:

(Zechariah 1:3) *"...Return to Me," says the LORD of hosts, "and I will return to you...."*

(Zechariah 4:6) *"...This is the word of the LORD to Zerubbabel: 'Not by might nor by power, but by My Spirit,' says the LORD of hosts."*

### FIRST DAY: Review of Daniel 10-12; Read Zechariah 1

1. What did you learn from last week's lesson about spiritual warfare?

2. The *"abomination of desolation"* was mentioned twice in Daniel 11 and 12. What is it and what prophetic information is linked to it? (See also Matthew 24:15-21.)

3. What verses in Daniel 12 refer to the resurrection of the dead?

4. Read Zechariah 1:1 Compare this with Haggai 1:1, Nehemiah 12:1-16, and Matthew 23:35. What facts can you state about Zechariah from these references.
   (a) Zechariah 1:1

   (b) Haggai 1:1

   (c) Nehemiah 12:1-16

   (d) Matthew 23:35

# LESSON 20
## PROPHETS OF ISRAEL

5. Read Zechariah's opening message in Zechariah 1:2-6. Try to summarize what he was saying in one or two sentences.

**SECOND DAY: Continue in Zechariah 1; Read Zechariah 2**

6. Zechariah received a series of eight visions that he was to describe to the returned exiles in Jerusalem. Read the first one in Zechariah 1:7-17. What specific comfort would this have brought to the people at that time?

7. Read the second vision in Zechariah 1:18-21. (Remember from our earlier study of Daniel that horns stand for kings and kingdoms.) What were the returning exiles supposed to be doing that would make the use of craftsmen as "heroes" significant in this vision?

8. Read the third vision in Zechariah 2:1-13 about the measuring of Jerusalem.
    (a) Consider what measuring usually means. Do you measure something you are going to throw away?

    (b) What are some common reasons for measuring things?

    (c) What do you think the measuring of Jerusalem was supposed to indicate to Zechariah about God's plans for it?

9. How was Jerusalem going to be protected as the population spilled over the old boundaries?

10. List some of the things that you learned from verses 6-12 about God's relationship with and plans for His returning people.

# LESSON 20

**PROPHETS OF ISRAEL**

## THIRD DAY: Read Zechariah 3

11. Read through the fourth vision in Zechariah 3:1-10. Compare Zechariah 3:1,2 with Job 1:6-12. What did you learn about Satan?

12. Joshua, the high priest, was the people's representative before God as well as the leader of all the priests and Levites in the active service of God. What do you think his wearing filthy garments, which were removed and replaced with clean, rich ones, was to symbolize to the returned exiles at this time?

13. According to verses 6 and 7, what must be done in order for God to allow His people to prosper in leadership?

14. What did God promise in verse 8? (See Isaiah 4:2 and Zechariah 6:12.)

15. If the stone with seven eyes in verse 9 represents Messiah (Jesus), how was the promise to remove iniquity in one day fulfilled? (See Zechariah 4:10; Isaiah 8:13,14; 28:16; Revelation 5:6.)

## FOURTH DAY: Read Zechariah 4

16. Read the fifth vision in Zechariah 4:1-4 and 11-14. Make a sketch below to help you visualize its details.

Page 111

# LESSON 20  PROPHETS OF ISRAEL

17. Read Zechariah 4:5-10. Reread Haggai 1:1 and identify Zerubbabel.

18. The task of rebuilding the temple was undoubtedly an overwhelming one. What wonderful word from the Lord did Zerubbabel receive
    (a) about his source for help in this?

    (b) about his being guaranteed success in finishing it?

    (c) about his awareness and appreciation of God's help when it was completed?

19. Read Zechariah 4:11-14. If Zerubbabel the governor and Joshua the high priest were symbolized by the two olive trees, what do you think the vision meant? [Remember that the seven-fold lampstand was a fixture in the holy place of the temple (Exodus 25:31-40).]

**FIFTH DAY:  Read Zechariah 5**

20. Read Zechariah 5:1-4. Describe what Zechariah saw here in the sixth vision. (**Note:** A cubit is 18 inches.)

21. (a) What two specific sins was God going to judge?

    (b) Comment on what would happen if this were the case today?

Page 112

# LESSON 20

**PROPHETS OF ISRAEL**

22. Read the description of the seventh vision in Zechariah 5:5-11.
    (a) Who was the woman in the basket?

    (b) What do you think was symbolized by her being carried in an ephah or bushel-basket which closed her in with a disc-shaped talent of lead as the lid?

    (c) Where did the women with stork-like wings take her?

    (d) Read Leviticus 11:13,19 for information about how God classified storks. How would this shed light on who was in charge of the woman?

23. Read Genesis 11:2-9, Daniel 1:2, and Revelation 17.
    (a) What is the significance of Shinar in the Bible?

    (b) What had happened there to Judah in the recent past?

    (c) What will happen there in the far future?

24. Look back over the first five chapters of Zechariah. Summarize three or four of God's revelations about Israel's future?

Page 113

# ZECHARIAH 1-5

## Which Zechariah?

At least twenty-seven different men in the Bible were named Zechariah, but details about the author of this book were given to distinguish him from all the others. This Zechariah was the grandson of the prophet Iddo, one of the priests who accompanied Zerubbabel when fifty thousand Jewish exiles in Babylon acted on the edict from Cyrus of Persia allowing them to return to Jerusalem (Nehemiah 12:1-4). So, by birth, Zechariah was a priest, in addition to being used by God as a prophet. His father's name was Berechiah, but Berechiah must have died rather young, because Zechariah was listed as taking his grandfather's place as head of the family among the exiles returning to Judah (Nehemiah 12:16). Also, at the time Zechariah received these prophetic visions and messages, the angel called him a young man (Zechariah 2:4). However, even though he was a faithful prophet from a young age, he was not exempt from the evil actions of others. Jesus remarked, in Matthew 23:35, that Zechariah was the last of the Old Testament prophets to be martyred, *"murdered between the temple and the altar."*

Zechariah was a contemporary of Haggai, and he dated his first prophecy just two months after Haggai's first message, in 520 B.C. They both were sent to exhort the exiles who were rebuilding the temple and the city of Jerusalem. Zerubbabel, the appointed governor of Judah, a descendant of the royal line of David, had been chosen to lead the return to Israel in 538 B.C. Once there, he had involved his people immediately in the rebuilding effort and succeeded in laying the foundation for the temple. However, after just two years, they all had become discouraged, not only by how much work there was to do but also by outside interference from enemies around them who successfully appealed to the reigning king of Persia to stop the work. For fourteen years the renovations had been discontinued, but God had not approved the delay. He stirred up His prophets Zechariah and Haggai to confront the leaders and people in Jerusalem about their disinterest in the work and to challenge them to begin again to rebuild the temple.

## Opening Message (Zechariah 1:1-6)

Zechariah jumped right into God's main message to the returning exiles: *"The LORD has been very angry with your fathers"* and has said, *"Return to Me...and I will return to you"* (Zechariah 1:2,3). The ancestors of the returning Jews had not paid attention to the warnings given them by God's prophets. As a result, they died, as did the prophets who spoke to them, while God's word was fulfilled down to the last detail. Calling God *"the LORD of hosts,"* which emphasized God's authority over uncountable spiritual forces, Zechariah proclaimed that God would continue to do just as He had promised. If the returnees continued to disregard His prophets, they could expect to meet the same end as their fathers.

## Horses among the Myrtles (Zechariah 1:7-17)

The record of the last couple centuries of life in Israel and Judah had been dotted frequently with accounts of outside invasions from enemy nations. Egypt, Assyria, Babylon, and even Edom had tormented and oppressed them. This first in a series of visions received by Zechariah in one evening spoke to that record. Zechariah was first shown a man on a red horse, in front of several others on different colored horses, standing among some myrtle trees in a hollow or shallow valley. Myrtle trees were short evergreen trees that bore fragrant white blossoms. Like olive and palm trees, myrtles were common in Israel and probably were used here to indicate that the spiritual forces were headquartered by God in the midst of His people. When Zechariah asked the man in charge what he was seeing as he looked at the horsemen, he was told that the horsemen were the ones dispatched by God to patrol and observe the earth. The riders reported to the Angel of the Lord, apparently the first man on the red horse to whom Ezekiel had spoken, that the earth was *"resting quietly."* To hear that the surrounding nations were at peace, even if the exiles faced a difficult time in rebuilding the temple, must have been of some comfort to them all. At least they were not about to be attacked!

Calming His people, then, seemed to be God's purpose in this first vision. Often, in Scripture, *"fear not"* was spoken first by God's messengers to His people in troubling situations, before they were told what they were to believe and obey.

The Angel of the LORD asked God the next question, perhaps because the contrast of the peaceful nations to the overwhelmed Jewish returnees was so great: *"How long will You not have mercy on Jerusalem and on the cities of Judah, against which You were angry these seventy years?"* (Zechariah 1:12). Evidently God had wanted the vision to arouse in them this feeling of tension over the seemingly undeserved peace of their former enemies in contrast to their own plight. God responded that He was zealous over the return and renewal of His people and their city, but He was very angry at the nations who were enjoying peace after they too-viciously carried out His judgment on Israel. He promised that He would return His mercy to Jerusalem and rebuild it, letting the cities of Judah *"spread out through prosperity,"* as He brought comfort to His people in Zion.

## Horns and Craftsmen (Zechariah 1:18-21)

Still in the same place in the same evening, Zechariah looked up to see another vision. This time he saw four horns. When he asked the angel who had talked to him before what they meant, he was told that they represented the powers that had scattered God's people. Their being four in number has caused speculation as to what powers they represented. They were probably not meant to be seen as the four world kingdoms mentioned in Daniel because verse nineteen indicated the horns had already scattered Israel, while two of Daniel's four kingdoms had not ascended to power yet. The four horns probably are best interpreted as representing the four-corners of the earth or all the enemies of Israel.

Next, Zechariah saw four craftsmen. He was told that the craftsmen had come to terrify the four horns and to cast them out. The word for craftsmen can be translated to mean any sort of workman, but in light of the temple-building project going on at that time, the craftsmen employed there may have been meant. How were these to "terrify" the enemy? Perhaps spiritual warfare was indicated: As Zechariah's peers continued in obedience to God's orders to rebuild the temple, God would keep the enemy away. The good work of the craftsmen would put the temple back in its proper place and position as God's house, so it again would become the place from which His light of truth could go forth to **permeate** a dark world and push back Satan's forces. Demons are terrified by the power of God displayed through His obedient people.

## Enlarging the City (Zechariah 2)

The third vision was of a man using a measuring line to measure the width and length of Jerusalem. Two angels conversed in this vision, and one was sent to explain things to Zechariah, the *"young man"* (Zechariah 2:4). The angel told him that Jerusalem would one day be so large in population that her people and livestock would spill out beyond the old boundaries. At that time, God would be *"a wall of fire all around her"* and the glory in her midst (Zechariah 2:5).

In light of this promise, God issued the command for the rest of the Jewish exiles to come out of Babylon. God planned to *"shake"* Israel's enemies and give the spoil of the victory to His people. He promised to be in the midst of them as a sign of His favor and a stimulation to their faith. He further assured them that many other nations would be joined with them in worshiping the Lord in that future time, too. Then, at last, the LORD would take back full possession of Judah and *"again choose Jerusalem"* (Zechariah 2:12).

[Note of interest: Right after the initial command to leave Babylon (Zechariah 2:6,7), two parts of the Holy Trinity seem to be conversing. Back in Zechariah 1:12, the Angel of the Lord, frequently believed to be the pre-incarnate Jesus, was said to have asked a question of the Lord of hosts. Here, in Zechariah 2:8, the Lord of hosts was speaking and said: *"**He sent Me** after glory, to the nations which plunder you; for he who touches you touches the apple of **His** eye."* Again, it appears that God the Father and God the Son are talking to each other. How interesting!]

God urged His people to *"sing and rejoice"* over their coming promotion (Zechariah 2:10), but He warned the rest of the nations to *"be silent... before the LORD, for He is aroused from His holy habitation."* When God comes in judgment, it will a time of great grief and shock for His enemies.

## Changed Garments (Zechariah 3:1-5)

In Haggai's prophecies, Zerubbabel, the governor of Judah from the line of David, had been singled out for praise because of his faithful leadership. Here, in Zechariah's vision, the high priest Joshua was featured in his position as spiritual leader of the people. In sort of a shocking scene, Zechariah saw the throne-room or courtroom of God in which Joshua, dressed in filthy clothes, was standing before God, with Satan opposing him and the Angel of the Lord defending him. The conversation between the Angel of the Lord and Satan was recorded and showed the Angel of the Lord using God the Father's name to rebuke Satan, much like Israel's war-angel Michael did in Jude 1:9 when they struggled over the body of Moses. This sort of glimpse into the spiritual dimension, which God had His prophets record from time to time, always seems a bit mysterious. While Satan's access to God's presence to accuse the saints is troubling, the presence of an **Advocate,** speaking in defense of them, is quite comforting.

In the vision, the Angel of the Lord (here again commonly thought to be the Second Person of the Trinity or Jesus) ordered the filthy garments removed as a sign that Joshua's sin was forgiven. He then ordered rich and beautiful robes to be placed on him, signifying forgiveness and restored purity. Joshua was even allowed to wear again the clean turban appropriate for his office as high priest (Exodus 29:6). As the representative of the nation and as their earthly representative before God, Joshua, in his new garments, symbolized the restored spiritual life of the nation.

## The Future Branch (Zechariah 3:6-8)

As the vision featuring Joshua, the high priest, continued, the Angel of the Lord promised Joshua that if he continued to walk in God's truth, keeping His commandments, God would let him succeed in his work and even honor him with a place among those in heaven. Evidently the presence of others in this heavenly vision, maybe people recognizable to Joshua and Zechariah, was important, as the Angel said, *"For they are a wondrous sign."*

God intended to do an even greater work than just raising up Joshua to spiritual leadership. God revealed to Zechariah something new. Sometime in the future, God would bring forth His own unique Servant (note the capitalization, indicating deity), whom He called *"the BRANCH"* (Zechariah 3:8). Isaiah had been shown this same future happening at a time when Israel would be regathered to experience a national cleansing: *"In that day the Branch of the LORD shall be beautiful and glorious; and the fruit of the earth shall be excellent and appealing for those of Israel who have escaped"* (Isaiah 4:2). Jesus, in the New Testament, spent most of his life in Nazareth; interestingly the word that means "the branch" in Hebrew is very similar to the word for Nazarene. Matthew 2:23 recorded this statement about the return to Nazareth after Joseph had taken Mary and Jesus to Egypt to escape Herod: *"And he [Joseph] came and dwelt in a city called Nazareth, that it might be fulfilled which was spoken by the prophets, 'He shall be called a Nazarene.'"* Isaiah gave another prophecy of this future leader in Isaiah 11:1: *"There shall come forth a Rod from the stem of Jesse, and a Branch shall grow out of his roots."* That gave the lineage of this Branch as the line of David, son of Jesse, further pointing to Jesus in its fulfillment. Jeremiah confirmed this with this prophecy:

> *"Behold, the days are coming,"* says the LORD, *"that I will raise to David a Branch of righteousness; a King shall reign and prosper, and execute judgment and righteousness in the earth. In His days Judah will be saved, and Israel will dwell safely; now this is His name by which He will be called: THE LORD OUR RIGHTEOUSNESS"* (Jeremiah 23:5,6).

national sin was being taken away, but ominously, in the vision, it was removed to Shinar or Babylon, from where, according to Revelation 17, the lid would one day be opened to have that same wickedness, so prevalent in financial trading, loosed to corrupt many more nations from that commercial center.

Zechariah's visions had given his audience much to consider. The work they were called to do in rebuilding the temple would further God's plans to present His Servant the BRANCH to *"remove the iniquity of that land in one day"* (Zechariah 3:9). Whenever we obey God and work faithfully on the tasks He has assigned us, we also take part in a work that affects things beyond the present moment. In light of this information, is it time for you to get back to such work?

## VOCABULARY

1. **advocate:** one who pleads in another's behalf, especially a lawyer
2. **capstone:** the top stone of a wall or other structure
3. **permeate:** to flow or spread throughout

# Notes